PELICAN BOOKS

PHILOSOPHY AND LIVING

BY

OLAF STAPLEDON, M.A., Ph.D.

(II)

PUBLISHER'S NOTE

PELICAN BOOKS

PHILOSOPHY AND LIVING

BY

OLAF STAPLEDON
M.A., Ph.D.

VOLUME II

PUBLISHED BY
PENGUIN BOOKS LIMITED
HARMONDSWORTH MIDDLESEX ENGLAND

Published in Pelican Books 1939

MADE AND PRINTED IN GREAT BRITAIN BY
HAZELL, WATSON & VINEY, LTD., LONDON AND AYLESBURY

CONTENTS

VOLUME II

CONTENTS

CONTENTS

CHAPTER VIII

PERSONALITY

I. SOME PSYCHOLOGICAL PRINCIPLES

(a) *Philosophy and Psychology.*—We have derived "good" and "bad" from the activity of conscious beings, the fulfilling of their capacity. We cannot give concreteness to these abstract phrases without making an excursion into psychology, the science of behaviour, and particularly of conscious human behaviour. Our concern with the physical sciences was only indirect, but psychology we must consider more closely. As the science of human behaviour, it should throw light on the proper fulfilling of human capacity. We shall examine it, however, from the philosophical point of view. Psychology is simply one of the sciences, and therefore a field for specialists, like physics or chemistry. Part of the philosopher's task in relation to all sciences is to study respectfully the findings of the specialists, so as to discover the bearing of one science on another; but also he must try to form clear ideas about the fundamental assumptions with which the specialists work, so as to discover if possible what their significance is, not merely for the practical purposes of the particular science but for philosophy.

What then is the philosophical bearing of the vast, incoherent mass of doctrines known as modern psychology? What of permanent value does it tell us of the nature of human personality and its healthy functioning ?

(b) *Psychological Determinism.*—The psychologist's aim is to discover principles which will enable him to predict human behaviour and control it, as the chemist predicts and controls the behaviour of atoms. The psychologist wishes to be able to declare that " human beings of a certain type, faced with certain circumstances, will behave in certain manners and can be influenced by certain methods." In fact, he wishes to show that human behaviour is systematically related to certain determinants in human nature and the environment. Only in so far as psychological determinism is true, only in so far as human behaviour is not arbitrary, can the psychologist go about his business at all.

We have seen that all scientists work inductively. From masses of data they construct formulæ descriptive of the general pattern of events. With these formulæ they predict future events with more or less success. Scientific laws, we have noted, are *expected* to hold good in the future; but we know no necessity why they should. At any time they *may* be broken. So far as we are concerned, electrons, if they do behave systematically, do so not because in the nature of things they must, but spontaneously, because they have it in them to behave in certain manners.

Psychological laws are on the same footing as physical laws, though they are much less precise, much less comprehensive, and much less reliable. They are descriptions of ways in which *on the whole* people of certain types behave in certain circumstances. For instance, in serious danger most people try to escape, unless they have some strong motive for doing otherwise. Owing to the complexity of human behaviour and the sketchiness of psychology, only the simplest and most obvious laws can be relied upon with any confidence; and these are all laws of a biological type, descriptive of the reactions of fear, sex, hunger, and so on. We shall later question whether these laws of primitive behaviour are adequate for a full and true description of human behaviour in all its modes.

Meanwhile let us note that, even if this is not the case, psychological determinism may still be true. Even if it is necessary to construct special laws for the more developed activities, human behaviour may still be systematic and therefore predictable. On the other hand, it might be found that this was not the case. There *may* be something absolutely indeterminate and arbitrary in human behaviour. It is at least *possible* that in some human acts there is a factor which is absolutely novel, something which is, in the fullest sense of the word, creative.

If psychological determinism is true absolutely, human behaviour is in theory predictable throughout. Should this possibility be contemplated with horror? No. In actual life the man whose conduct is recognised to be systematic, predictable, reliable, is valued and praised, not spurned, so long as the determining principles of his conduct are themselves good principles. A deterministic system of psychology which described just how, just with what degree of moral integrity, different kinds of men would behave in different circumstances need not be disheartening, so long as it allowed generous and noble motives to be in some considerable degree actually effective, and not merely disguised resultants of the interaction of primitive impulses.

The only kind of freedom that matters is not freedom for completely irresponsible, arbitrary caprice, but the freedom which consists in *self*-determination, in contrast with determination by something external to the self, or something within the self but less than the *whole* self. In the act of falling down a precipice a man is relatively unfree, since the event is almost wholly determined from without. In walking he is relatively free, since the event is largely determined by his own active nature. On the other hand, if, under the impulse of obsessive hate, he walks to commit a murder, contrary to his better judgment; if, in fact, his act is determined by an insistent partial motive, although he knows that it will lead to disaster for his self as a whole, then he is in an important sense less free than if he resisted the temptation. Finally, even in an act of prudence, if its motive is obsessive self-regard in conflict with the considered will to behave socially, a man may be said to be less free than in self-abnegation for an end which he himself recognises as more worthy than self-preservation. In this kind of act he achieves the highest possible degree of freedom. That is, though his act is fully determined, it is determined in accordance with his own fully conscious and fully integrated will. In fact, he himself determines it, acting, of course, in relation to the external world. He himself, no doubt, is a determinate something. He has a certain nature and not some other nature. But in so far as his act was a complete and unrestrained expression of his own nature, he was free, in the only sense that matters; even if, in turn, his nature was in the past determined by influences other than himself which produced him.

(c) " *Mental Chemistry*."—The analytical method, which proved so useful in the physical sciences, was naturally applied in psychology. In this field, of course, it has proved immensely useful; but it has also been responsible for a good deal of unsound theory.

David Hume, as we have seen, regarded the mind as a stream of " impressions and ideas." Some of the followers of Hume claimed that to understand this stream of consciousness we must analyse it and discover the laws which determine the patterns and sequences of the elements which compose it. They thought in terms of " mental chemistry." Consciousness at any moment was like a very complex and everchanging chemical compound made up, so to speak, of mental atoms. Further, they believed that one fundamental principle underlay all psychological laws, namely the principle of " mental association." The present experience, they said, tends to recall features of past experience which were *associated* with this particular kind of experience on past occasions. Thus the visual appearance of an orange as a round, yellow, mottled patch recalls the fragrance and sweetness that were formerly associated with such visual experiences. The psychology based on this principle is called Associationism, and is fundamentally " atomistic." It deals in mental " atoms."

These " mental atoms " are supposed to consist of unit characters of sensation—units of colour, pressure, warmth, sound, and so on, occurring in patterns to form shapes, physical objects, rhythms; and capable of being recalled as images from past experience. Some of the patterns are supposed to be intrinsically pleasant or unpleasant, others acquire pleasantness or unpleasantness in relation to the primitive need of the organism to preserve itself, or to its more sophisticated needs, acquired in a civilised environment.

As we shall see, the theory is open to many serious objections, which are of two main types. The first is that the mind is not " built up " of unitary elements. It is essentially an " organic whole," in which every part is determined by its relation to the rest. The second objection is that the mind is not simply a passive recipient of impressions. It is essentially active, or (if you prefer the word) dynamic; and its experience is largely determined by its activities or its capacities for action. Let us consider the unity of the mind.

(d) *The Unity of Experience.*—The mind, then, is not made up of mental atoms which are distinct and self-complete and unmodified by their relations with the whole of experience. The mind is not built of separate bricks. Experience is not composed of mortared units. It is " seamless." Its parts fade into one another. Moreover, everything in experience qualifies and penetrates everything else. Whatever we experience is experienced in virtue of its difference from other things. A perceived shape, for instance, is a determination within the total visual field. It is what it is in virtue of the background which it is not. Warmth is sensed in contrast with cold, light with darkness. We perceive patterns, which closer attention can analyse into their component parts. We do not build the patterns up out of mental elements. In this connection one of Professor Köhler's experiments is significant. He confronted a hungry ape with two cards of different shades of grey. Behind the darker card there was food, behind the other nothing. After a few such experiences the ape learned to go straight to the darker card. But one day the light card was removed and a fresh card, darker than the original dark card, was put in its place. In the altered situation, the ape chose the new and very dark card. That is, it was all along reacting, not to a particular shade of grey, but to " darker," as opposed to " lighter." On the atomistic theory it should have continued to respond automatically to the original, medium shade, no matter what other cards were introduced.

We must conceive of the infant's mind not as a " buzzing confusion " (to use William James's phrase), but as a shifting, unsteady experience of very simple patterns against a very vague, unnoticed background. Its mental progress consists of gradually filling out the patterns with detail, by analysing out their features ; and in the progressive discovery of fresh patterns in the hitherto unnoticed background. Probably the infant does not even distinguish between the different sensory fields. Its mother is not something which occurs in the field of sight, *and* in the field of touch, *and* in the field of sound. She is simply a seen-felt-touched thing.

In this connection we must distinguish between what Bertrand Russell has called the " psychologically primitive " and the " logically primitive." The psychologically primitive is what comes first in the development of the mind, the vague perception of unanalysed physical objects, actually composed of elements from several senses. The logically primitive is the detailed pattern of unitary sense-characters which the expert mind reaches by careful analysis of common-sense perception of physical objects. For the understanding of the physical world, what matters most is the logically primitive. For the understanding of the mind, both are important, in different connections. Even for the understanding of the physical world, it is important to realise that the unitary sensory characters, which the expert discovers by the analysis of perception, are not the absolutely fixed, discrete elements which they were once supposed to be. Every sense-character is intrinsically related to others by contrast. The seemingly atomic structure of experience is not strictly atomic.

Our present concern is the mind, and its unity. We must never lose sight of the fact that the mind, whatever it is, experiences things *together*. When we see a dog and hear it bark, there is not merely the seeing a dog *and* the hearing it bark. There is a single experience of " see-hearing." Seeing we hear, and hearing we see. And each factor of the single experience to some extent modifies the other.

The unity of experience is particularly striking in the relation of knowing, feeling, and striving. These were formerly regarded as distinct faculties which might function independently of one another; but every mental event really involves all three of them, or rather has three aspects. It is a case of know-feel-strive, or (in technical language) cognition-affection-conation. Obviously there can be no conscious striving that is not a striving about something known and felt. There can be no feeling (liking or disliking) that is not feeling about something known and striven for or against. There can be no knowing that is not itself an enterprise, an activity, a striving, either to grasp or to avoid something. Moreover, in another way also knowing involves striving. Our knowing, our cognition, is determined not only by the objective world but also by our interests. These direct our attention hither and thither, and actually modify our knowing.

The atomistic or granular theory of experience is faced with a peculiarly striking difficulty in respect of memory. If it is taken seriously it makes memory impossible. According to the theory a particular act of memory is just a system of mental imagery to which is attached a feeling of " pastness." It has also certain relations within a wider system of possible imagery, similarly toned with " pastness," namely " my past experience." But within the terms of the theory it is quite unintelligible that memory should be *about* actual events which formerly occurred and are now non-existent. For if it *is* about actual past events, the conscious act of remembering must be something more than a *mere* present event having no contact with the past. Something or other that *was* present at the past event must persist now. Such a *spanning* of past and present the theory does not permit. So far as the theory is concerned, memory must be a gigantic illusion. I may have come into being a few seconds ago equipped with a complete set of bogus memories which have no relation to a real past. If we insist on believing that memory really reports the past we must refrain from describing consciousness in such a way as to make this impossible.

This difficulty over memory is a good example of the limitations of the analytic method. We must distinguish between " aggregates " and " organic wholes." An aggregate is a collection of independent things, such as a heap of stones. An organic whole is a system in which the nature of the parts is determined by their relations with the rest of the system. Animals, minds, and works of art are organic wholes. If you analyse an organic whole into parts and regard the parts as discrete self-complete things, and then explain the whole in terms of them, your explanation will be superficial.

We must now ask whether there is really any truth in the doctrine of Associationism. No doubt in some sense a present experience tends to " recall " similar experiences in the past, and also their associates in the past. But how can this be explained in terms of the theory ? If the factors of experience are wholly distinct from one another, how can mere likeness constitute a *link* between them ? Is similarity a sort of magnetism ?

If on the other hand we think of experience, not as a patchwork and succession of separate things, but as the complex activity of a single enduring thing, this difficulty is avoided. We should then describe association thus. When the " enduring thing " is stimulated to act in a certain manner (e.g. seeing an orange) in which it has acted on former occasions, it tends to be in some degree aware of the former act and of the whole pattern of activity (e.g. fragrance and taste) in which the former act was a member.

What of this " enduring thing " ? If it is to serve the purpose of the explanation, must it be a substance, with changing attributes ? Before dealing with this problem let us very briefly consider the observable nature of the individual mind and the ways in which minds differ.

II. THE DYNAMIC INDIVIDUAL

(a) *Perception, Memory, Thought.*—First let us remember the second main criticism of the old Associationist psychology, namely that the mind is not passive but essentially active. We have already seen that cognition (which includes every kind of apprehending) is determined partly by the object cognised and partly by the dynamic nature of the individual. His needs and interests direct and limit his attention. His sense-organs can respond only to a few of the innumerable kinds of stimuli that flood in on him. No sense-organs, for instance, are adapted to " radio " waves, or ultra-violet waves, or super-sonics. Only stimuli of those kinds which have proved relevant to biological need are selected by specialised organs.

Another important character of our mental life is that it includes immediate acquaintance with change. Experience is always " going on." It does not consist of a durationless instant of present experience which " clicks " into the past. If it did we should have no *perception* of change or movement. But we do actually *perceive* things moving and changing. Our present is therefore a span of time, not a timeless instant. One event fades into the next and gradually ceases to be present.

Next, sense-experience is filled out with vague sensory imagery derived from the past, so as to afford perception of the hosts of three-dimensional physical objects of the world of ordinary life. Past experience can also be recalled as explicit memories with a feeling of " pastness," and more or less precise location in the system of remembered and merely " heard-of " past events.

231

The most striking difference between human cognition and that of even the most developed sub-human animals is that in man there is a far higher degree of the power of abstraction, of forming general ideas, or (more precisely) of attending to the universal characters that large classes of events or situations have in common, while ignoring the idiosyncrasies of the particular events or situations. Professor Köhler's chimpanzees, as we have remarked, abstracted the character that renders packing-cases climbable. Man goes much farther in abstracting such very general characters as " a million," " justice," " space," " truth." The power of abstraction has been immensely aided by the practice of using verbal symbols, or names, to earmark and signify particular things and universal characters. Without language, thought could never have passed far beyond the stage reached by the apes. Unfortunately, like all potent instruments, language is dangerous. Symbols may come to lose their meaning, or take on several meanings. Such debased symbols, or pseudo-symbols, which have no objective meaning at all though they are manipulated as though they were genuine symbols, may lead to all manner of superstitions and subtle unconscious confusions of thought.

Men vary greatly in cognitive powers. Some have better sensory equipment than others. Some can discriminate differences which are too slight for others to detect. In fact, some are more capable of analysis. Some, on the other hand, are better at synthesis. They have, so to speak, wider mental grasp. They can detect the relationship of facts which superficially seem to have no connection with one another. Such powers as these go to make up the complex capacity known as intelligence. Clearly some individuals are more intelligent than others, either in special fields or in every field. Some, for instance, have more " practical intelligence," some more "theoretical intelligence." Some are specially gifted with intelligence in the sphere of personal intercourse. They are peculiarly apt at detecting slight changes of mode in the behaviour of their fellows, and responding appropriately.

These cognitive powers, though they may vary in degree in different individuals, are common in some degree to all. Besides these powers we must allow the possibility of others which the average man lacks, or has only in a negligible degree. There is some evidence that at least a few individuals, perhaps all to some extent, are capable of " telepathy," of direct access to the experience of others, without the mediation of the senses. This conclusion is at least strongly suggested by recent experiments. Still more surprising, experiment has also seemed to support the claim that some are capable of " clairvoyance," of " extra-sensory " perception of physical facts which could not be reached either by the normal channels or by telepathy. Such claims need to be supported by a much greater mass of evidence before they can be accepted as fully established; but in the present state of human knowledge it would be foolish to rule out the possibility of such powers. It is, after all, very probable that our present naively materialistic knowledge touches only the fringe of reality. Supernormal modes of cognition may actually occur amongst us; and they may constitute a fragmentary hint of powers proper to a higher plane of evolution.

(b) *Straining Toward Action.*—We must now consider the individual as a centre of feeling and striving, and we must begin with another criticism of Associationism. Any particular present experience must have an immense number of very diverse associations in the past. What is it that determines which of all these shall actually be recalled? For the hungry man all sorts of experience are apt to be reminiscent of food; all trains of thought lead sooner or later to memories or fantasies of feasting. Yet when he has fed, his attention will wander in other directions. The course of association, and indeed the character of perception itself, are largely determined by the claims of interest or need. After a visit to Switzerland an artist and a geologist will give very different reports of the country. The one will see the mountains mainly as complicated coloured shapes, the other as geological formations.

The individual is essentially dynamic. He is doing things and straining to do other things. Biologically and psychologically he is a system of needs to act in specific manners in response to the state of his own body and the environment. When he is empty, he needs to seek food. When in danger, he needs to escape. When sexually ripe he needs to make love. When thwarted by another living creature he needs to take violent hostile action. And so on. These needs or active behaviour-tendencies or dispositions largely determine his cognition of his world. He is far from a merely passive recipient of external fact.

For psychology, as for biology, the most significant concept is that of the active organism, responding to the stimuli of the environment. The organism must be regarded not simply as a physical thing, but rather as a body-mind, as something to be studied both from the physical and the psychological points of view.

We must be careful not to suppose that a need, or disposition, or behaviour-tendency, is a hidden bit of machinery which *compels* the organism to behave in a specific way. When we say that a man needs food or tends to eat when he is hungry, we are not expounding an internal necessity; we are merely summarising a host of observations of particular cases of human behaviour. Even when we attribute some particular behaviour to some hidden need, we are doing no more than describing. If, in the manner of the psycho-analysts, we derive (let us say) a particular vindictive act from repressed father-hate, we are only saying that the act has characters in virtue of which it must be assigned to a certain class.

Though a need is not to be thought of as a hidden bit of machinery, we must nevertheless think of it as in some sense a disposition (momentary or constant) toward some *specific* kind of activity, a potentiality of acting in a certain manner in response to a certain kind of situation. On the other hand, we must beware of regarding dispositions as inflexible, unalterable, distinct factors; and the personality as a tissue woven of these harsh fibres. Rather we must think of dispositions as all, in varying degrees, fluid or viscous, as only relatively constant. In fact they are intrinsically related parts within the organic whole of the personality.

The individual's activities are teleological. They are determined by a goal or end, at least in the sense that, when a certain end is attained, the activity ceases. For instance, in flight from danger, the course of

235

activity may vary with circumstances, but when the individual has escaped the danger, by whatever course, flight ceases. We must be careful not to confuse the end which actually causes quiescence and the biological end which an observer is tempted to consider the true end of the activity. Thus the actual end of eating is a filled belly, but the biological end is supposed to be nutrition. Biological ends are those which seem plausible on the theory that all behaviour is directed in the main toward the survival of the individual or the race. The actual end is simply the observed end-state of a series of acts.

(c) *Innate and Acquired Need.*—In many sub-human animals behaviour is mainly an expression of the inherited nature of the individual. It is but slightly modified by experience. Insects perform complex stereotyped actions without having to learn them. If the normal environment is altered, they show only very slight power of readjusting their behaviour. The nest-building of birds is less complex and more adaptable, but clearly it also is mainly innate. In the higher mammals behaviour is much less precise and rigid. It consists mainly of very general types of activity in response to very general types of situation. They are responses partly to a condition of the external world, partly to a condition of the organism itself. Eating, for instance, involves not only the presence of food but an organic condition. Very roughly the kinds of innate activity may be catalogued as: nutrition, escape, defence, attack, sex, parenthood, and gregariousness. All are directed toward some actual end-state, but within limits their course varies with the detail of the environment. In the higher sub-human animals all are modifiable by experience. Through trial and error, or more distinctively intelligent insight, animals can learn modes of behaviour very different from the innate modes.

In man the innate is still more vague and more flexible. Behaviour is modified to a still greater extent by intelligence. Nevertheless, under the influence of the revolt against rationalism, some psychologists have claimed that the innate factor is all-important for understanding human behaviour. All our actions, they say, are determined in the last analysis by innate dispositions to act in certain manners in response to certain stimuli. Sometimes these innate factors are regarded as mental entities and called instincts; sometimes instinctive action itself is said to be at bottom a case of mere physiological reflex action, like involuntary sneezing, though of course much more complicated. Of the instinct-psychologists one school inclines to emphasise the sexual instinct as by far the most important determinant; another stresses self-regard; another postulates a general instinctive urge which is directed hither or thither according to the environment's impact; while others claim that man's instinctive nature must be analysed into a large number of innate dispositions, such as fear, anger, sex, protectiveness, gregariousness, self-assertion, curiosity, manipulation, vocalisation, and so on.

There can be no doubt that there is an innate basis in all our behaviour, and that it is not unlike that of the higher sub-human animals. But the attempt to describe all human behaviour as simply a subtle expression of instinct is misleading. There is no clear knowledge of the innate factors; and to explain human behaviour in terms of them is to explain the known by the unknown. In man, save when he is acting under stress of violent primitive emotion, the primitive needs are overlaid by such a complex system of acquired needs, or learned habits of action, that they are of little use for explanatory purposes. Almost any concrete action may afford some satisfaction for almost every innate disposition (or reflex mechanism), and can be plausibly accounted for in terms of each of the conflicting theories.

Clearly, then, though we must recognise that at bottom human nature is very much like (say) ape nature, and that in primitive situations man often acts in an almost purely " animal " manner, we must also recognise that in typically human and civilised situations all his behaviour is much more complex, and demands for its interpretation not only concepts derivable from the study of animal behaviour, but also concepts derivable only from human behaviour.

(d) *How Behaviour is Modified.*—The commonest way in which new modes of behaviour are acquired, both in men and animals, is by the process known as " conditioning." When a dog smells food, gastric juice flows into its stomach. If the smell of food is many times accompanied by the sound of a bell, and then finally the bell is sounded without the presentation of food, the gastric juice flows in response to the bell alone. If every time a baby is shown a bowl of gold-fish a pistol is fired behind it, it will in time become terrified by the mere sight of gold-fish. If in men's minds a certain idea is frequently associated with a certain emotional stimulus, the emotion *may* come to be felt in relation to the idea itself, quite irrationally.

Thus a political policy, even if it is foolish, may come to seem attractive merely by being associated with free drinks and motor rides, or with an adored leader. Reason may then be brought in to justify the attractiveness and prove the policy wise.

The other method by which behaviour is modified in men, and much less frequently in other animals, is the method of intelligence, which we have already examined in the cases of the chimpanzee and Einstein. This is the distinctively human way, though some behaviour of sub-human animals shows rudimentary intelligence, and most human behaviour is almost wholly the product of mere conditioning.

It should be noted that, even when intelligence has worked out a new method of behaviour, the new method may not be adopted. Well-established habit may prove irresistible. On the other hand, if the new behaviour *is* adopted, intelligence need not come into operation again whenever the behaviour is repeated. A *new* automatic habit may be formed on the basis of the new behaviour. The chimpanzee, having intelligently solved the problem of the suspended fruit, may come to perform the necessary actions in future without repeating the painful act of intelligent insight. The multiplication table, once learnt in laborious processes of reasoning, may be repeated parrot-wise.

Our daily life consists of an immensely complicated system of habitual actions, intermittently modified by conditioning or by intelligence. Washing, dressing, catching trains, going about our business, making love, disputing, fearing calamity, longing for success, contemplating our own nature and the world's, these and a thousand other actions are carried out by each of us in the distinctive manner characteristic of his unique personality. All may be regarded as expressions of his innate psycho-physical nature modified by the impact of the world, and in turn helping to form his future nature.

(e) *Hierarchy of Activities.*—One thing at least is clear about human behaviour, namely that some activities are more complex than others. Compare, for instance, a sneeze, a stroke in tennis, the decision to embark on a certain career, life-long devotion to a public cause. Of these cases we may say both that some are experienced by the agent himself as more complex than others, and that some, objectively studied, are observed to involve in fact more complex capacities than others. Thus, to take an extreme case, the intelligent desire to embark on a certain career involves considerable knowledge of society and of one's own aptitude, whereas a sneeze involves no more than a simple reflex mechanism. Deliberate conscious activities may be said to vary in respect of the " knowing " involved in them, the " feeling " involved in them, and the " striving " and actual " doing " involved in them. These three aspects, as we have seen, are inseparable. There is no " knowing " that is not a " striving," and so on. But for the understanding of a particular bit of behaviour one aspect may be more important than another.

It is arguable, though there is not agreement on the subject, that along with differences of complexity in behaviour there also appear differences of quality. In this view love, for instance, which includes the realising of another person as a centre of conscious activity, and also the self-neglectful cherishing of the other, is not

fully accounted for by describing it as a highly complex
form of response to stimulus, of the primitive biological
order. It seems to involve a kind of apprehension and
feeling and striving not reducible to the primitive.
Before accepting any account which claimed to describe
these higher activities wholly in terms of primitive
activities we should have to make certain that the
distinctive features of higher activities had not been
overlooked or misrepresented.

Very roughly, and without deciding whether the distinctively human activities are " reducible " or " emergent," we may classify the hierarchy of behaviour as
follows:

(1) Simplest of all, though even these are incredibly
complex, are the purely physical and chemical reactions
of the physical units of the body, considered as a
purely physical system. It may or may not be that a
complete account of physical behaviour can in theory
be given solely in these terms. For my part I am quite
ready to believe that it can. But at the same time I
should insist that this purely physical and therefore
very abstract account of behaviour would be less
significant for the understanding of human nature than
the account given in humanistic terms.

(2) Next come the simplest vital reactions of individual cells, considered as minute living things. These
are overwhelmingly more complex than the sub-vital
physical reactions of the physical units in inorganic
situations.

(3) Far more complex again are the simple reflexes,
such as the shutting of an eyelid in response to the
presence of a foreign body in the eye. In all such
action, we are told, there is a train of physiological

events which consist of: (*a*) stimulation of a sense-organ (fly in eye); (*b*) passage of a nerve-current along a sensory nerve-channel into the spinal chord or the base of the brain; (*c*) continuation of the current along a more or less direct course linking the sensory to the relevant motor nerve in the central nervous system; (*d*) passage of the current outwards along a motor nerve to the relevant muscle or gland; (*e*) contraction of the muscle or chemical action of the gland. In simple reflex action the response is very stereotyped, but it can be conditioned to new stimuli, as in the case of the dog's gastric flow. Experiment strongly suggests that emotional states are produced by, or through the medium of, certain chemicals in the blood, and that these chemicals are produced by special glands which are set in action by reflex mechanism. Thus anger is correlated with the presence of adrenalin, which is produced by the adrenal gland by reflex stimulus in response to " anger situations." Adrenalin injected into a cat makes the cat angry. Mere water does not.

(4) Simple reflexes may occur together or in sequences to form compound reflexes, such as standing, digesting, breathing. These also may be conditioned.

(5) " Instinct " may be merely a case of very complex and highly flexible or modifiable " compound reflex," in which the whole action is controlled by special emotion reflexes. But we must allow for the possibility that instinctive action really involves a novelty over and above reflex action. However this may be, though in the human infant there are purely instinctive (or reflex) actions, such as sucking and rage, in the grown man,

and even in the child, very little unmodified " instinctive " action occurs. Rage, for instance, is roused not only by physical resistance, as in the animal, but by all manner of conditioned stimuli resulting from civilised life (e.g. the receipt of a letter). Even the response itself seldom takes the primitive form of physical attack. It may, for instance, consist of writing another letter.

(6) We come now to the hierarchical rank which includes the distinctively human kinds of behaviour and experience, the kinds which are characteristic of man, though they are spasmodically and precariously attained by the highest sub-human animals. The simplest example of this is practical intelligence. Human behaviour is to a greater or less extent modified by the power of coping with novel situations not merely by trial and error but by noticing their relevant features and relating these with significant features of past experience. As we have seen, the essential character of this behaviour is the act of attending to likenesses and differences, and thereby abstracting universal characters, which can then be manipulated in imagination for experimental purposes. This power of forming " free ideas," and performing imaginary experiments with them is not only the source of practical intelligence and of intellect but is also an essential factor in imaginative art and in imaginative insight into self and others. Indeed, it is this power which enables the passage from mere habit-formation to the formation of " sentiments." In habit we respond to a stereotyped situation with a familiar stereotyped action. A " sentiment," on the other hand, may be defined as a complicated system of responses varying in relation to

243

Thus the child personifies not only its doll but all striking physical objects. The savage personifies not only his fetish but winds, trees, rivers, rocks. Even the civilised adult tends to personify lifeless objects that receive much attention. The shipmaster personifies his vessel, the engineer his machine. We are all in danger of personifying abstract ideas and large groups of individuals. The religious devotee personifies almightiness and love. The patriot personifies the State or the People. These are all cases of misplaced transference of the reaction *proper* to persons, or at least to conscious beings.

We must distinguish between two very different ways of reacting to persons, one primitive, the other more developed. In the primitive mode, though one recognises the other as a person, as a conscious being, one reacts to him only as a means for fulfilling one's own needs. In the more developed mode one wills the fulfilment of the other's needs in the same direct manner as one wills one's own fulfilment. Further, as we distinguish between impulsive acts of self-assertion (such as anger) and the established sentiment of self-regard, which may issue in all sorts of action, so also we must distinguish between impulsive affection and established sentiments of other-regard. Impulsive acts of affection occur not only in human beings but also in sub-human animals in relation to mates and offspring. In John's behaviour toward Jane, then, we should distinguish between (a) impulsive acts of self-assertion and affection, and (b) the established sentiments of self-regard and Jane-regard.

It is perhaps worth while to point out that any concrete act may happen to be at once impulsive and an expression of a sentiment; and further that it may express both the self-regarding sentiment and other sentiments. Indeed, so complex and so unified is the human individual that almost the whole of his dynamic nature may express itself in a single act.

Having contrasted genuine other-regard with the primitive reactions toward other individuals, let us now contrast primitive gregariousness with the distinctively human attitude toward society. Roughly we may say that primitive gregariousness, as sometimes seen in herds of cattle, consists in a set of stereotyped responses to stimuli. Isolation from the herd produces reactions of anxiety and the attempt to return to the herd. Danger produces clustering, and some degree of unity of action. Eccentricity in any individual produces hostility on the part of others. On the other hand, the exceptionally powerful and masterful individual is reacted to with submission, and is followed.

Genuine human sociality, on the other hand, is so different from this that any attempt to explain it as " merely " a development of primitive gregariousness is far more misleading than significant. Of course even human sociality *is* mainly of the primitive type; but civilised and truly human social behaviour does occur, and plays an immensely important part in small groups of individuals in personal contact. In large groups, not cemented by personal contact, it is very much more precarious and rare, but it is at least a potent ideal. Genuinely human sociality is rooted in the distinctively human power of realising other individuals as conscious persons, and willing their needs without ulterior, self-regarding motives. But it is more than a sentiment for particular cherished individuals. It is in fact the deliberate will that all individuals, known and un-known, within the society shall be treated as persons, not merely as manifestations of the herd. The society in question may be of any size, from the family or the city to the nation or the whole human race. But the larger and less coherent the society, the more precarious is the sway of true sociality.

Personality is essentially social. A human being completely isolated from his kind throughout his life would be less than human. Without social intercourse, without stimulation by contact with other individuals, and without cultural heritage, he would be at best a rather quick-witted beast, more probably an imbecile. So intimately do personality and community interpenetrate that we must devote a chapter to the consideration of this problem alone. Meanwhile, several other aspects of the individual's nature must be considered. I will close this section by explaining a phrase which I have already used more than once, namely " creative activity." I use this phrase to refer to any kind of activity which raises the mental life of the individual temporarily or permanently to a new and higher level of development, in respect of sensitivity or of integration. It may be that very many kinds of activities are to some slight extent " creative " in this sense, but I use the word rather to mean those activities which are *in the main* of this kind. Thus, some education, some art, some intellectual work, some personal intercourse, deserve the adjective " creative."

(*f*) *Conflict and Repression.*—A man's needs very often conflict with one another. The world being such as it is, the fulfilling of one need often makes the fulfilling of some other need impossible. Conflict may take place either between needs of the same hierarchical rank or between needs of different ranks. Of the first kind would be a conflict between impulsive pugnacity and impulsive fear, or, on a higher level, between love and hate of the same person. On the other hand, in a conflict between, on the one hand, the will to catch a train so as to fulfil an important engagement and, on the other hand, an impulse to have a drink on the way, the needs are of different rank. The most dangerous conflicts, on the whole, occur between an end which the individual cherishes as most important or sacred and any primitive and deep-rooted impulse which threatens to violate it. Conflicts of this sort can cause profound discord and cleavage in the personality. For instance, a child's conflicting impulses with regard to its parents may cause permanent disorders in its mind.

Freud, whatever his mistakes, has a great achievement to his credit. He has shown that in such cases of grave conflict the disreputable impulses, intolerable to the dominant personality, may be " repressed " into " the unconscious." That is, needs or cravings which are gravely inconsistent with the ideal of personal virtuousness may be resolutely ignored. The individual may cease to be able to attend to the fact that he has such cravings at all. If consciously he admires and loves his father and " unconsciously " he needs to be rid of him or get the better of him, the disreputable need, though not recognisable, will not cease to be a factor in his nature. It will express itself by distorting his feelings and thoughts not only about his father but about anything which is superficially identifiable with his father or the relation of parenthood. In fact, to use the jargon of psycho-analysis, it will generate " in his unconscious " a " complex " with regard to his father.

A complex may conveniently be regarded as a senti-ment the object of which is not valued consciously or disvalued consciously. The object *is* valued (or dis-valued), but it is impossible to attend to the fact. The individual is actually " set " in favour of the object (or against it), but he is not aware of the fact. Neverthe-less, because he is set in that direction his conscious activity is to a greater or less extent influenced in that direction; and this influence, from the point of view of conscious ends, is irrational.

Sometimes conflict takes another form. The re-pressed matter, instead of remaining as a submerged and distorting influence, may capture for a while the stronghold of consciousness. Either the subject's tem-perament may suddenly and dramatically change, so that to his friends he becomes " almost a different person "; or, still more strikingly, this emotional change may be accompanied by a loss of memory of his whole past career, so that he becomes in a more literal sense a new personality. In this new state he may continue for years. Or he may undergo repeated alternations of personality, or even spawn a number of subordinate personalities.

Such cases are rare, but none the less significant for the understanding of the nature of personality. Far commoner, and seemingly universal, is the distortion of thought and will by repressed needs.

III. THE UPPER REACHES OF HUMAN PERSONALITY

The foregoing account of the hierarchy of human activities was purely descriptive. No attempt was made to find in one particular level the explanatory principles for the understanding of all the levels. Some materialists would have us believe that if we had a complete account of the atomic structure of the human body we should be able to predict all its actions in terms of physics. The Behaviourists in America, for instance, regard the reflex as the key to the under- standing of all behaviour, and the reflect they assume to be reducible to purely physical terms.

Some psychologists, on the other hand, do not believe that such an explanation is possible even in theory. As we have seen, they insist that human behaviour cannot be understood save by means of the concept of purposive or teleological activity; and physics, of course, has no place for teleology. Desire and thought do not fall within the scope of purely physical laws. These psychologists, as we have seen, have attempted to classify what they regard as the basic teleological dispositions or instincts, and they claim that even the most subtle behaviour is in fact simply an expression of primitive instincts acting in much disguised forms. We have already noted that there is not much agreement as to what precisely the basic instinctive dispositions are.

It has therefore been argued by critics of " instinct psychology " that, after all, instinct is not a very useful concept for the understanding of human behaviour. While some seek to reduce instinct to reflex, others seek to show that instinct itself is too mechanical a concept for the explanation of the upper reaches of personality. Some claim that the most significant con- cept is the sentiment, in the psychological sense. Of course any organism's behaviour is an expression of its own nature in response to the environment; and its nature is in the first moments of its life purely innate. All the same, what is innate in it is simply a capacity for behaving in a certain manner *in a certain environment*. The organism cannot behave *in vacuo*. Organism and environment co-operate in behaviour. Further, from the first moment onwards the influence of the environment changes the organism's nature; and the more sensitive and flexible it is, the more it is changed. The more developed the species the more subtly is each individual " keyed into " the environment; the more, that is, does the environment itself affect the organism's constitution, moulding it, and creating in it, or at least evoking in it, new capacities not logically reducible to the laws of the behaviour of a simpler organism in a different environment.

If this view is correct, a man's behaviour is not to be understood in terms of any one level of behaviour. It is an expression of all his levels, interacting in a complex environment that stimulates them all. The attempt to explain behaviour by purely physical laws or purely physiological laws, or by laws of pure instinct, is doomed to failure. One might almost as well turn the tables and try to explain it all in terms of aspiration toward the divine.

Perhaps we have been unduly dogmatic. Perhaps we should say only that *in the present state of knowledge* it is not possible to describe human behaviour in terms of any one level; and that our failure suggests not merely a lack of sufficient data but an insufficiency in our explanatory concepts. Perhaps the key to the problem lies on none of the levels but in some much more general principle which correlates all of them but cannot yet be formulated.

We must remember, too, the possibility that ultimately, although a complete account of physical behaviour may be given in purely physical terms, *yet* for a real understanding of human nature the purely physical may be too abstract an explanatory principle.

However this may be, all that we can do in our present ignorance is to study each level on its own merits, formulating its special laws, and " reducing " these laws to lower-level laws only when this can be done without falsifying the facts to be explained.

For instance, in explaining the growth of sentiments we may reasonably affirm that in the first instance the object of the sentiment is simply a stimulus to various kinds of instinctive activity. Jane, for instance, is a stimulus to John's sexuality, self-regard, gregariousness, protectiveness, and so on. But as attention is increasingly focussed on the sentiment's object, so that it is realised as a conscious person, a new mode of behaviour is evoked, not describable in terms of the simple concept of instinct. Jane creates in John the capacity for taking Jane herself as an end. Between this new capacity and the lower-level capacity there is constant conflict. And much that passes for higher-level activity is really lower-level activity masquerading. To the unprejudiced mind, however, this makes no difference to the fact that higher-level activity does occur.

It may be objected that all our assertions about the higher reaches of personality are so vague as to be worthless. To this we must reply that inevitably they are vague, since their subject-matter is very complicated, and psychologists have as yet seldom faced it without prejudice. But it is better to make a few significant though confused protests than to be content with an over-simplified theory.

I shall now try to suggest what these " upper reaches " of human personality actually comprise, so far as we can as yet ascertain.

Some claim that telepathy and clairvoyance and pre-vision of the future are high-level powers characteristic of the upper reaches. I am not in a position to judge whether such powers exist or not, though on the whole I incline with much hesitation to believe that in some form or other they do. But I cannot see anything particularly lofty about them. They may be *consequences* of high development, but in themselves they are merely strange modes of perceiving events of common-place order.

On the other hand, it is fairly clear that under the heading of " personal sensibility " we do exercise powers that involve the upper reaches of human nature. The core of the matter, as we have seen, is the realisa-tion of another individual as an active conscious per-son, and the disinterested willing of his fulfilment. This apprehension opens up a whole new world of perception and of action which is distinctively human, in that the sub-human has no access to it. It is a world known in some slight measure to all of us, though only those who are specially gifted with personal sensibility are at home in it. Literature is largely concerned with it.

We may reasonably suspect that in creative art, and most obviously in the tragic ecstasy, expression is given to the higher reaches of personality; of course along with most other levels. No satisfactory theory of æsthetics has yet been devised, nor even a satisfactory psychology of artistic activity. Æsthetic experience in its most developed form eludes all descriptive explanation, and affords a sense of novel awakening and lucidity. It is reasonable, therefore, to believe that it entails activity of the " upper reaches." In fact, as was said in the chapter on ethics, æsthetic experience can be most satisfactorily described in terms of the symbolic fulfilment of impulses of every level, sensory-motor, instinctive, personal, social, and probably mystical also.

Intellectual activity itself is, of course, distinctively human. It involves a power of abstraction which could not be predicted from the psychological study of purely sub-human creatures. But even in its dizziest flights it exercises nothing more than the initial power of abstraction, though, of course, greatly improved. It belongs to the " upper reaches " only if we interpret the phrase to apply to all that is distinctively human, not if it is to exclude all but the powers at the extreme limit of human capacity.

The same should perhaps be said of " personal sensibility " if it were not that this phrase may be taken to cover a wide range of activities from simple apprehension of the other as a discrete conscious individual to much more subtle (and less describable) experiences of the other as in some manner an embodiment of universal powers.

If there is any truth in the concept of the " upper reaches " as consisting of capacities at the highest limit of human development, we should include under it certain experiences and powers which may be called mystical. To say this is not necessarily to accept all the interpretations which mystics give of their experiences. I shall discuss this subject in a later chapter. It is extremely unlikely that *any* interpretation couched in language derived from normal experience can be true of " upper range " experience. Description must necessarily work by means of conceptual thought, and this was moulded under the influence of normal mundane experience. It may be that the reports of the mystics have all a certain extremely metaphorical truth, at least for those who have some immediate acquaintance with the experience described; but to the rest of the world such descriptions are likely to be wildly misleading.

For my part, and speaking mainly with reference to such traces of seemingly mystical experience as have happened in my own life, I hazard the suggestion that the essence of the experience consists not in discovering new truth but in taking up a new attitude, an attitude which I can only describe as one of delighted or even ecstatic acceptance of the universe.

IV. DIFFERENCES BETWEEN PEOPLE

Our sketch of human nature would be seriously incomplete if we made no reference to the differences between individuals. The more complex an organic species the more scope there is, all else being equal, for differences between its individuals, since there are more respects in which differences can occur. No doubt in gross bodily respects dogs vary more than men, but the mental differences between men are probably far greater and more complicated than any differences between dogs.

Differences between individuals are in part an expression of innate factors, in part the result of differing circumstances. Though the influence of the environment may disguise and even reverse innate characters, these are important determining factors throughout life. In studying the differences of individuals it is difficult and sometimes impossible to decide how much is innate and how much acquired; but for our present purposes we may ignore this problem and consider merely how people do actually differ.

We may start by distinguishing between differences of degree of development and differences of capacity on the same hierarchical plane. The former may be called " vertical " differences, the latter " horizontal." The distinction, of course, is not fundamental, but merely a convenient method of study. Though accurate measurement is still impossible, we cannot but recognise that some individuals manifest higher general development than others. On the whole they are more sensitive in all directions, and more capable of discriminating slight differences. In all respects they are more intelligent and also more integrated, more capable of acting in relation to their experience as a whole, less distracted by passing impulses which they themselves, in calmer moments, would regard as trivial. The fact that it has proved very difficult to estimate differences of this kind must not blind us to the fact that in daily life we recognise them. In extreme cases they are flagrantly obvious.

Though particular differences of temperament and capacity are on the whole to be regarded as " horizontal " differences, there are certain capacities which belong distinctively to the higher levels of development, since on the lower levels they may be almost negligible. Of these I will mention, without staying to define them, sensibility to personality, social responsibility, capacity for dealing with human beings, capacity for abstract thought, certain kinds of artistic capacity, and the capacities which with some hesitation I have called mystical.

Of the " horizontal " differences between people much might be said, but space forbids. We may very roughly distinguish differences of special capacity and differences of general temperament. Of special differences we may note that, for example, some have and some have not outstanding musical ability, or mathematical ability, or ability for draughtsmanship, or for the use of words, and so on.

Temperamental differences are much more difficult to distinguish. The old classification of individuals into melancholic, sanguine, choleric, and phlegmatic is probably not so superficial as was recently supposed. Without attempting to discover the essential factors of temperamental difference, we may note at random that some are more sociable, some more solitary, that (quite apart from ability) some have more theoretical and some more practical interests, that some are more interested in human beings and some in lifeless matter, that some are more intuitive and some more ratiocinative, that some are in general more cautious, conservative of their vital resources, while others are more venturesome and spendthrift.

Many attempts have been made to systematise such differences as these. For instance, there is the famous and useful distinction between the introvert and extravert temperaments, the former on the whole meditative, inward looking, seeking mental tidiness or coherence, the latter active, outward looking, seeking constant intercourse with the environment. Another distinction that has been suggested is that of cerebrotonic, viscerotonic, and somatotonic, between those who live mostly in the brain, those who live mostly for the emotional life which is controlled by glands and nerve-ganglia in the viscera, and those who live mostly in the body as a muscular system, and are therefore addicted to sport and physical exercise.

Here we need not pursue the difficult problem of classifying and explaining temperamental differences. I mention the subject only to suggest that human minds are in fact immensely different from one another, that they are generally quite unconscious of the real nature of their differences, that their intercourse is therefore often extremely jarring and bewildering, that in spite of superficial similarities one type may find it almost impossible to understand and sympathise with another type, and may incline to condemn the other as barbarian or inhuman, while in truth the one is just as human as the other.

In this plight our only hope is to try as far as possible to become aware of our differences, so that we can make allowances for them, seeking so far as possible to enter imaginatively into the other's point of view. For differences should become a source not of enmity but of mutual enrichment.

V. WHAT IS THE SELF ?

One question about human personality we have not yet properly faced, and though it seems to some the most important of all questions, I shall only briefly discuss it. Is " the mind " or " the self " simply the stream of experiences that goes on from birth to death, or is there an enduring something, an " ego " or essential mental substance which *has* the experiences ?

There are two main types of theory about the nature of the self. Professor Broad calls one kind " central theories " and the other " non-central theories." In central theories there is a central enduring self *to* which experience happens. The centre may be conceived either as a unique mental substance (a " metaphysical ego "), or as " the body," or as a central core of enduring experience, including the internal body-sensations. Of these three possibilities I shall speak only of the " ego " theory; since the other two reduce either to the " ego " theory or to some kind of non-central theory. In non-central theories experience is a centreless tissue or flux. The former type may be represented by a wheel with axle and spokes, the latter by a net.

The main arguments for the " ego " theory are: (1) Common sense assumes a centre, and claims that we are literally *self*-conscious, that we have introspective acquaintance with the " ego." (2) Some unifying principle is needed to provide the ground of the unity or mutual interpenetration of experiences, and particularly the interpenetration of past and present experiences in memory. (3) If, as Realists claim, experiencing is essentially a relation between an experiencer and an experienced, there must *be* an experiencer, just as there must be an experienced object.

The main arguments for the non-central theories are: (1) We have *no* introspective acquaintance with the " ego." As Hume long ago said, when we seek to discover the self, we only come upon particular " impressions," or in modern language particular experienced objects, such as sense data of the body. (2) The unity of experience, it is claimed, can be satisfactorily accounted for without a substantial self to do the unifying. Indeed, if the unifying principle is thought of as a substance, it cannot fulfil its purpose. A second principle must be invoked to provide a link between the single, constant substance and its innumerable fleeting experiences. The correct method (we are told) is to describe the unity of the mind as the unity of a *system* of a special kind, in fact an organic whole, in which the parts are *intrinsically* related to one another. (3) Experiencing is indeed a relation between an experiencer and an experienced, but it need not be a relation between a unique unanalysable substance and the objects of experience. It might be a relation between a system of events and some fresh event assimilated to the system. Thus, when I perceive a pear, certain sense data are brought into mental relation with the system of mentally related past events which constitute " my mind." In this view successive states of consciousness are not the acts of an enduring substance; they are events having a very special relation to one another. As William James said, each thought is born an owner of preceding thoughts, and dies owned by the following thought.

It is impossible to do justice to either of these points of view in a short space. I mention them merely to indicate the kind of problems that have to be faced in any attempt to study the nature of the self. My own impulse in this controversy, as in many others, is to " have it both ways." That is, I suspect that both kinds of theory, thoroughly worked out, would arrive at essentially the same conclusion, which would be a theory having some characteristics derived from both the simpler theories. Some indication of the general type of a satisfactory compromise-theory may be found in the following suggestions. It is a mistake to abstract and hypostatise either the unity of the mind or the plurality of its components. The mind is not a single substance " having " mental events. It is entirely analysable into its mental events, even if some of them are " unconscious " or not open to introspection. But on the other hand mental events are not distinct atoms or bricks out of which a mind is built. Each of them is intrinsically related to the rest of the mind. In fact they, no less than the unique, unifying "ego," are abstractions.

In the light of the tentative findings of this chapter and the chapter on Immortality, we may, I think, draw a rather important conclusion. It is a two-fold conclusion. On the one hand we must not regard the human individual as being in some manner precious merely on account of his individuality; for his individuality is probably not the simple eternal thing that some suppose it to be. On the other hand the human individual is the ground of all that is to be prized, within the limits of our experience. From one point of view the importance of human individuals is apt to be overestimated, and from another point of view underestimated. It is not the individual as such that matters, but the vital, mental, spiritual activity which constitutes him. He matters not because he is himself, but because he is capable of knowing-feeling-willing, and particularly because he is capable in some degree of the most developed kind of knowing-feeling-willing, which can be very roughly summed up by the old words " reason " and " love." Because this is so, the whole aim of society should be to enhance the capacity of individuals for the life of reason and of love.

CHAPTER IX

COMMUNITY

I. Problems of social philosophy. II. Two theories of the nature of society. III. How men behave in groups. IV. Prerequisites of genuine community. V. Prospects of community in the modern world.

I. PROBLEMS OF SOCIAL PHILOSOPHY

WE have seen that personality is an expression not only of innate structure but also of environment. In the case of human personality the environment is very largely social. In some sense human personality is through and through an expression of present and past social environments. But precisely in what sense? We must now face this problem, which is one of the two main problems of social philosophy. On the one hand lie theories according to which individuals alone are " real," and society is merely the system of related individuals. On the other hand lie theories according to which society alone is " real," or " fully real," and individuals are mere abstractions from the concrete social whole. Between lie theories which compromise by suggesting that both society and individuals are abstractions, and that neither should be hypostatised. or regarded as an independent self-complete entity; but that, taken in their actual relation, both may be called " real."

From these various types of social theory emerge various types of social ideal, ranging from extreme individualism to the apotheosis of the State.

When we have discussed these traditional problems,

we shall examine in more detail the nature of community, and its pre-requisites. We shall consider also its prospects in the world to-day.

In the next chapter we shall turn to the other great problem of social philosophy, namely the search for the underlying principles which determine social change and social evolution. This will involve us in a discussion of the Marxian theory of economic determinism.

II. TWO THEORIES OF THE NATURE OF SOCIETY

(a) *Individualism.*—The philosophical individualism of the eighteenth and nineteenth centuries was a system of ideas appropriate to a commercial class that was rising into dominance through individual enterprise in industry and commerce. The triumph of the doctrine is a good example of the determination of thought by economic influences.

According to the theory, individual men and women are self-complete realities or substances, and " society " is the mass of them in relation to one another; or (in another sense of the word " society ") the abstract system of relations which holds between them. In this sense, " society " as a whole, including every one of its multifarious institutions from fashion to marriage, from the club to the State, is simply a very complex system of manners in which individuals behave toward one another. According to the individualistic theory, individuals are to be thought of as " atoms," entering into, but not constituted by, their relations with one another.

Each individual, according to the theory, is regarded as a centre of experience and rational behaviour. Apart from aberrations due to ignorance, stupidity, or distorting passion, each seeks to preserve and advance his own person. When he behaves altruistically he does so because, through one cause or another, and indeed most mysteriously, his self-interest has been extended to include the self-interest of others.

The theory is associated with the doctrine of Utilitarianism, according to which, as we have seen, pleasure is the sole good, and the ideal is the greatest happiness of the greatest number. This ideal sets the true direction of all social activity. Nothing is to be sought but the pleasure of individuals, and one individual is as good as another, save that some may be capable of more pleasure than others, and some may be more useful to their fellows. The function of the State is to interfere with the free behaviour of individuals only so far as this is necessary in order to prevent them from hurting one another.

Hence the doctrine of Laissez Faire. It was confidently believed that the uncontrolled economic activity of individuals seeking private gain by competing to satisfy the demand for goods would ensure the greatest possible production, and also the just distribution of goods, and therefore the greatest possible happiness of the greatest number of individuals. It was assumed that on the whole people would demand the kind of goods which would most benefit themselves, and therefore society, and that production would be guided solely by the spontaneous demand of the masses of freely demanding individuals.

As we know, events did not justify the theory. Our concern is philosophy, not history; but it is impossible to see Individualism in its true light without noting how it worked out in practice. Those who had economic advantages were soon able to dominate society. Those who lacked advantages sank to the status of wage-slaves, to drag out their lives often in incredible misery and brutishness. Their distress was generally regarded as a necessary though regrettable consequence of the triumph of the system. Combination of the workers to wrest better conditions from the masters was condemned as a wicked interference with sacred economic laws. Little by little, however, the workers themselves, aided by a few generous individuals in the employing class, did compel the State to interfere more and more (by means of Factory Acts, etc.) to protect wage-slaves against wage-masters. Always such interference was regarded by individualists as a very dangerous practice, to be adopted only in urgent cases.

The faith that people would demand the kinds of goods which would most benefit them was falsified by three facts that the advocates of Laissez Faire overlooked. First, people did not really know what was good for them in the long run. Second, even when they did know, they were led astray by primitive cravings which were exaggerated to the pitch of obsession by the nerve-strain caused by unfavourable conditions. Third, capitalist propaganda and advertisement tended to stimulate these cravings rather than the desire for " the good life." The result was the tragic futility and vulgarity of our civilisation.

Along with economic individualism there grew up a morality which was individualistic not merely in the sense of being convenient to selfish individuals, but also in the sense that it was a social doctrine based on the importance of individual rights, individual responsibility, and individual intelligence and conscience. Individual rights were, of course, the only rights, and they were to be curtailed only to safeguard the rights of the majority of individuals. Freedom of action and of speech became basic political values to be safeguarded and increased. This was admirable, but it was overlooked that to the wage-slaves political freedom was useless without economic freedom. Complementary to individual right was individual responsibility. Since the individual was real, and society an abstraction, the individual must think for himself, and must will according to his own lights, never surrendering his intelligence or his conscience to the care of other individuals. In the sphere of religion the rise of the " Nonconformist Conscience " was an expression of the general feeling for individualism. In our day, when individualism has become an unfashionable doctrine, we tend to forget that it was not merely the glorification of selfishness, and that it contained much of permanent value.

Unfortunately the worse elements of the theory tended to be put in practice more than the better. Selfishness ran riot; individual responsibility was too often evaded; liberty was not preserved. Freedom of action and of speech did not include freedom on the part of the wage-slaves to act and speak against their oppressors.

The fact that Individualism as a practical political and social policy has had regrettable results constitutes in itself no condemnation of Individualism as a theory of the nature of society. But it not unreasonably arouses suspicion and an inclination to seek some theory in which society appears as more real than its individuals and as imposing a special obligation upon them. Of course the advocate of Individualism may reasonably argue that, if effective provision were made to ensure that all individuals should have an equal chance, the policy would work. To this it may be replied that even if a society of individualists were to be put in this state of very unstable equilibrium it would very soon generate a dominant class which would use its advantage to fortify its own position.

(b) *The Apotheosis of Society.*—At the other extreme from Philosophical Individualism lies the political theory associated with Philosophical Idealism. For Kant and his followers, particularly Hegel, the whole was necessarily more real than the parts. This theory, as we have seen, is derived from the theory that all finite things, including finite minds, are *constituted by* their relations with other things. So far as human knowledge is concerned each thing simply *is* the system of its relations with the rest of the universe. Of the things in themselves which have those relations nothing can be known. It is merely postulated as the one, universal, Absolute Reality. Of finite things (we are told) it may with human and partial truth be said that the more comprehensive a thing, the more real it is, since it approximates more to the Whole which alone is fully real.

The application of this theory to the nature of society was very striking. In a very important sense an individual is an expression of the society in which he occurs. His every act is determined by his biological inheritance, his own past experience, and his present environment. There is nothing whatever in him (according to the theory) that is not social or racial through and through. The form of his whole life and every moment in it is, so to speak, an expression of society's willing and thinking in and through him. The only thing about him which is not determined from without is the abstract and completely featureless capacity for experiencing in *some* manner and acting in *some* manner. *What* manner depends wholly on his social, historical, and biological " location " so to speak.

The Idealist philosophers were not greatly concerned with biology, but we may significantly give their theory a biological interpretation to bring it in line with contemporary thought. Biologically the individual inherits the dispositions for the special modes of behaviour characteristic of his species and his unique individuality. These dispositions are themselves determined by the pressure of past environments working on the indeterminate potentiality of his ancestors, selecting some biological strains rather than others. Even if, as we are told, natural selection cannot account for the occurrence of the variations themselves, nevertheless, whatever their source, it must be a source beyond the finite individual that manifests the variation. It is a social and a racial source. In fact, according to the theory, it is the Absolute Reality, of which all particular things are merely particular aspects.

Apart from biological inheritance, the individual mind is determined by the social tradition in which it is nurtured. As we have seen, all a man's experience is limited by the categories which traditional culture imposes on him. Or rather, he can only transcend his traditional culture in so far as contemporary social circumstances or the special conditions of his life compel him to do so. The creative originality of the individual need not be denied, but it may be thought of as the " spirit of the whole " possessing him and acting through him. His originality consists in some special sensitivity or insight into the nature of his experienced world, and a consequent imaginative leap to new modes of behaviour more appropriate than the old modes. But this special sensitivity itself is the product of past social and racial factors.

Some philosophers, bearing in mind all these considerations, have been led to a sort of deification of society or the race. An extreme case is the theory of the " group mind." It is well known that in a crowd or mob individuals may behave quite otherwise than they would in isolation. Seemingly the " spirit of the crowd " possesses them and imposes on them its own forms of feeling and of thought. Each individual is carried away by the enthusiasm or passion of the crowd, so that he willingly participates in acts that may be either more brutal or more generous than he or any average individual in the crowd could have performed without the support of the crowd. Lynching mobs, patriotic assemblies, revivalistic religious congregations, afford evidence of these statements. Less dramatic, but to some minds equally impressive, is the spread of fashionable ideas in a national community. Like the wind on a cornfield, some mysterious force seems to sway all minds together in unison, with spreading waves of thought and feeling. Should we not, then, say the advocates of the " group mind " theory, think of society as a great brain made up of individual cells ? Must we not believe that all individuals, though they seem to themselves to be living their own mental life in isolation from one another, are in fact possessed by a common, unitary social consciousness ?

Many Idealist philosophers who did not accept the theory of the " group mind " in this extreme form adopted a theory very much like it in effect. In their view a mind was essentially a system of ideas and valuations, a system of " mental content." The whole of the individual's " mental content " was merely a minute excerpt from the total system of ideas which constituted the whole cultural life of society. This mental content of society as a whole they regarded as real independently of the individual minds that participate in it; and indeed as more real than the individual minds, since it was vastly more comprehensive.

Just as Individualism triumphed because it was congenial to a rising commercial class, so theories which hypostatised the State or the race flourished because they were congenial to a class that had secured power and regarded its political and social institutions as essential to the life of the community. Just as Individualism produced its characteristic morality, so did the theory that we are now discussing. We have already seen that in Idealist ethics the moral claim is the logical claim of the individual's " real " will over his actual and merely partial will, and that his " real " will is the completely rational and good will, which is said to be identical in all individuals, and is the will for the greatest possible fulfilment of society as a whole. In this theory, what is really best for the individual himself is that he, with his particular capacities, should be used to the best advantage by society for the social good. It followed that the right course for the individual was not, as the individualists declared, to seek his own interest, in the faith that in this manner he would best serve society; on the contrary he must serve society, in the faith that in this manner he would fulfil his better, his " real " self.

Further, since he as an isolated individual had no reality, since he was a mere abstraction from the concrete whole of society, he must not presume to set himself up as a judge of society's morals. Since his thought was but a fragmentary abstraction from the whole culture of society it would be folly for him to judge that culture in the light of his private intelligence. Since his conscience was but an imperfect mode of the public conscience, it would be wicked for him to judge the accepted morality in the light of his own moral intuitions. For him the sum of righteousness must be to conform to the precept, " My station and its duties."

On the other hand, though for the average individual the right course was simply to fulfil his social function in the office to which fate had assigned him, some individuals there must be who were gifted with special powers of insight into the needs of society and the potentialities of cultural growth. These were the natural interpreters of the General Will, the true brain of the social organism. Without their mediation and guidance the masses would blunder into all kinds of folly and conflict. Obviously this doctrine was well suited to an established oligarchy which regarded itself as the rightful rulers of society.

Oddly enough the same kind of doctrine is also suited to a revolutionary party that claims to have a mission to remake society, and needs for its heroic task strict intellectual and moral discipline, and conformity to the dictates of the party. Marx turned Hegel back to front not only, as we shall later observe, in converting his form of idealism into a corresponding form of materialism, but also in re-stating for the purpose of revolution a moral doctrine that was originally well adapted to an established oligarchy.

Doctrines which hypostatise society have a special advantage which individualism has not. They can give a quasi-religious satisfaction, a sense of participation in and service of a supernatural being whose purposes are of a higher order than the purposes of individuals. This is their strength and their danger. For dangerous they are. They breed a fatal tendency toward a vague mysticism of State or race. They tempt self-assertive individuals to regard themselves as semi-divine leaders of society, and to mistake their own private advancement, and their own private prejudices, for the sacred will of society. They also afford to these self-styled interpreters of the general will an excuse for every kind of tyranny and ruthlessness. On the other hand, they encourage the average mentally lazy individual to shirk his intellectual and moral responsibility, to accept ideas and values uncritically, either from popular " leaders of thought," or from a vague and illusive public opinion, or from the official propaganda of the class that controls the great modern organs of propaganda. The ordinary citizen thankfully surrenders his intelligence and his conscience into the hands of others, and becomes a blind instrument.

But the fact that these doctrines are dangerous does not necessarily mean that they are false. Let us now try to judge both the social theories that I have been describing, both Individualism and the Idealist political philosophy, in order to discover, if possible, what is good in each.

(c) *Synthesis.*—The Idealists' criticism of Individualism is in the main true, but their positive assertions go much too far. There is indeed good reason to hold that the individual's will is an expression of his biological inheritance and his social environment. Biologically the only qualification is that at every stage of his ancestry, no matter how remote, there must always have been something internal, something upon which the environment worked. Without that initial something, even though it was probably from the physical point of view just a very complex and unstable molecule, there could have been no biological evolution. And the offspring of that initial something, made more and more complex by generations of evolution and of intercourse with the environment, is man, with his highly-developed subjectivity.

Socially also a qualification must be made. Though the individual is through and through an expression of past and present society, yet, whatever his causes, he actually now is what he is, namely a particular and determinate individual, a centre of experience and action. To call him a *mere* abstraction would be false, if by " abstraction " is meant something non-existent. To " abstract " is to attend to a particular character while ignoring others. Though the character attended to is an " abstraction," it is not less objective than the whole of which it is a member. Of course, the human individual without a social environment would be a very different creature; but though the social environment profoundly influences his mind it is not essential to his mind's existence as a mind. Moreover, however he was made, there he *is*, a real centre of mental and physical activity.

Society itself is simply the individuals that compose

it. The individuals, of course, are organised in complex social relations, and are infused by their society's tradition and culture; but there is nothing that is society or the State over and above the individuals, with their present relations, and their traditions. Their relations are ordinary physical and mental relations between individuals. Their tradition is embodied in a huge mass of verbal and other symbolism, created by past generations of individuals, and interpreted by the present generation. Nowhere is there any evidence for a supra-individual self. Even the striking facts of crowd-behaviour can be fully explained without any such hypostatisation of the group. The individual in the crowd may be regarded as indulging in a particular sort of instinctive response to the special stimulus of the presence of his fellows. His reaction is what the psychologists call " primitive passive sympathy." He tends to manifest emotions and actions similar to those manifested by his fellows.

We must reject also the less extreme view which, though it does not postulate a group mind as an actual conscious process embracing all individual minds, yet regards the individual as a mere excerpt from the objective tissue of ideas which is the life of society. This view depends on the theory that a mind is simply a system of mental " content," of thoughts and values which can be identical in different minds. It ignores the individual mental activity which *has* this content, which thinks and feels it. *If* a mind is simply a system of " content," and a minute excerpt from the whole mental " content " of society, it follows that society is actually a mind of the same order as the individual's mind, though far greater. Against this view we must insist that the individual mind is of a different order from the tissue of ideas which constitutes culture, just as a tree is of a different order from a forest. From the Idealists' theory it follows that, since the whole is more real than the part, the social mind is more real than the individuals that compose it. But this view we have rejected. The parts even of an organic whole are not less real than the whole. A hand is not less real than the man, though it is less complete, and cannot exist in isolation, and is instrumental to the whole man.

Society, of course, the whole system of individuals, is more important than any individual or group of individuals, simply because it is *all* the individuals. It is always possible, no doubt, that, from the point of view of the welfare of the whole, a particular individual or group of individuals may be supremely important, or at any rate more important than others. But their enhanced value is instrumental to the whole.

We must admit that in a society composed of individuals of very different mental rank, say men and animals, or supermen and submen, the welfare of the men (or supermen) should count for more than the welfare of the animals (or submen), simply because they would be capable of activities and fulfilments of higher order. But actually the individuals of human societies do not differ in rank in this extreme manner. It is quite impossible to grade them in a mental hierarchy which will be demonstrably and objectively correct. Consequently, for political and social purposes, however much they may vary in social usefulness, they should be treated as though all were equally capable of mental fulfilment, as having equal claims to the consideration of society, and equal rights to express their will about the conduct of society, and, in the last resort, to determine its policy.

On the other hand, we must not fall into the errors of individualism and the cruder sort of democracy. We must recognise that the mass of individuals in a society, nurtured in unfavourable conditions, doomed to crippling activities, and educated not for responsibility and integrity, but for mechanical efficiency and docility, may be quite unable to recognise what is really best for them as individuals capable of mental development, and quite incapable of judging public policy. We must recognise, in fact, that a policy based on the expressed demands of the majority of individuals may lamentably fail to satisfy the deeper needs of those individuals themselves.

This fact must not be made an excuse for authoritarianism on the part of an enlightened minority. We have to-day plenty of evidence of the tyranny to which this inevitably leads. Instead, the enlightened minority must work by reasonable persuasion and the example of its own personal integrity and responsibility, till the masses recognise them as appropriate leaders. Unfortunately it is always easier to gain recognition and power by deceitful and emotional propaganda, and to secure it by coercion.

III.   HOW MEN BEHAVE IN GROUPS

(a) *Degrees of Social Awareness.*—Having considered the problem of the status of the individual and of society, we will discuss the different manners in which individuals are aware of society. The reader must be warned, however, that in this section I shall not be summarising well-established philosophical theories, but tentatively putting forward ideas which academic philosophers might regard as outside the province of philosophy. It will be obvious that in formulating these ideas I have been influenced by the writings of Mr. Gerald Heard, but I have also, for my own purposes, modified his theories in some very important respects. Mr. Heard speaks of the " evolution of consciousness " from the pre-individual type, through the individual type, to the fully social type; but I cannot determine whether he is describing different kinds of attitudes taken up by the individual toward society or different forms of a communal consciousness or group mind. In what follows I shall discuss merely the attitudes taken up by the individual to his social environment.

There seem to be three different kinds of mental attitude or three kinds of mentality which the individual may manifest toward the group of which he is a member. For brevity I shall call them the herd-mentality, the individualistic mentality, and the mentality of genuine community. All three attitudes are actually manifested by all extant human beings, at one time or another, or all together; but since some individuals are on the whole more prone to one attitude than the others, we may perhaps very roughly classify individuals according to their habitual attitude to society. And since we may with some confidence arrange the attitudes in order of mental development, we may similarly grade the individuals in respect of development of social consciousness.

I cannot believe, as Mr. Heard does, that it is possible to trace in history a gradual evolution from a condition when the herd mentality, the most primitive social attitude, was overwhelmingly dominant to a condition in which the most developed will for true community is intermittently occurring. Instead I incline to believe that the three attitudes have been common ever since our species emerged from the sub-human, and that throughout the historical period the individualistic attitude has been commonest. On the other hand, it may well be that in the highest sub-human mammals, and even in the earliest, most primitive human races, the herd-mentality dominates. It may be that in a biological type higher than our own the dominant mentality would be that of genuine community. But again it is not inconceivable that even in the case of *Homo Sapiens* more favourable social and economic conditions and better education may in the long run immensely strengthen the rudimentary community-will in each generation, and that in time even the imperfect nature of our species may be conditioned to genuine community.

However this may be, there are to-day three distinct ways of feeling about social groups; and if we wish to understand the nature and potentialities of human society we must form clear ideas on this subject. I shall now try to describe these social attitudes and I shall argue that the more developed cannot be described simply in terms of the less. Individualism contains a factor not reducible to herd-mindedness; and genuine community-will contains something not reducible to individualism.

(b) *Herd-mindedness.*—The most primitive social mentality is illustrated most strikingly in typical mob-behaviour. The individual is intensely conscious of the presence of the crowd as a vague surrounding mass, but much less aware of distinct individuals, save as focal points in the crowd. His attention is directed to individuals only when they become in any way significant of the mental life of the crowd, for instance by assuming leadership over him, or by being singled out as aliens, recalcitrant to the common mood. Even leaders and aliens fail to impinge on the mind of the crowd-member as real individuals. They are merely stimuli evoking in him a stereotyped response. He tends to be oblivious also of his own individuality. So far as he is self-conscious at all, his desire is to conform to the behaviour of the crowd. He is almost literally hypnotised by the crowd's presence.

Not every member is reduced to this state. On the contrary a few may react with heightened self-consciousness and self-assertion. But all *tend* toward herd-mindedness, even if some resist the tendency, and react in a contrary manner. Under the influence of a crowd-leader who senses the disposition of the crowd, and can express it, and within limits control it, the members eagerly conform to the prevailing temper. They allow their individual intelligence and moral sensibility to fall into abeyance. They accept uncritically such simple thoughts and feelings as can be communicated in the atmosphere of the crowd. Relatively simple, primitive, and emotional ideas can be communicated much more easily than ideas that are more subtle and less emotional. It follows that under the influence of the crowd each individual tends to be reduced to a mental level lower than his normal level, and is capable of actions which in the normal state he would dismiss as foolish or barbarous or base.

It would be unjust to say that in crowd-behaviour the

individual always tends to be less moral than normally, for skilful leaders can sometimes rouse a crowd to a high level of moral enthusiasm. But always this enthusiasm is evoked by some relatively simple and vivid moral experience, such as the saving of a life, or a protest on behalf of those who are oppressed. And such moral behaviour is far less common in crowds than a decline of moral consciousness.

Herd-mindedness does not occur only in crowds in which the members are physically present to one another. In every group which is regarded as an object of value there is a tendency to herd-mindedness. Tribes, families, cities, colleges, schools, aristocracies, class-conscious plutocracies, class-conscious proletariats, trade-unions, religious bodies, and above all nations may exercise this hypnotic power. We must, however, distinguish between the group's emotional dominance over its members as an object of veneration, as in the nation infected by patriotism, and the state of affairs in which, though there is no sentiment for the group, the individual is constantly drenched by the group's ideology and insulated from the ideology of other groups. Even the most independent-spirited individual may be gravely led astray by the sheer weight and detail of the social tradition in which he is drenched.

(c) *The Individualistic Mentality.*—The attitude which I have called herd-mindedness is obviously the psychological aspect of instinctive gregariousness. The individualistic attitude, on the other hand, is not simply the psychological aspect of instinctive self-assertion, though this instinctive reaction does, of course, fortify it. The individualistic attitude is more developed than any purely instinctive response. It involves not only instinctive self-assertion but also a fairly high degree of self-consciousness. The individualist, of course, is aware both of himself and of others as individuals. But whereas his self-consciousness is relatively persistent, his other-consciousness, his awareness of his neighbours as centres of knowing-feeling-striving, is intermittent and vague. Of course he may have impulses of affection for those who are psychologically nearest to him, just as he may on the plane of herd-mentality. He may even have enduring sentiments for particular individuals; and these sentiments may sometimes be genuine love-sentiments in which the other is valued not merely as a physical object is valued but as a person, whose well-being is desired for its own sake. But his dominant attitude toward his fellows is that of concentrated self-regard, and even his love-sentiments are apt to have a strong aspect of sheer self-regarding possessiveness. Indeed, in so far as his loves really are *loves*, in so far as they are genuine other-regard for a more or less clearly conceived person, he has passed beyond the limitations of individualism. As an individualist, though he is vaguely conscious of others as individuals, he is not impressed with a sense of their vivid reality. His dominant motive is the advancement of himself as a person among other persons. It does not follow that he is particularly " selfish." Indeed he may be ostentatiously generous. If he has been brought up to admire altruism, he may take as his ideal of personal advancement a pattern of Christian kindliness. None the less his mentality is essentially individualistic, in the sense that subconsciously he does what he does not for love but for personal salvation. Of course his beatitude may not be conceived as beatitude in life after death. It may consist wholly of gratification here and now for his need for self-respect.

The individualistic mentality is probably the dominant social attitude in all races, though all of us are at all times faintly herd-minded, and some are sometimes predominantly so. The genuine community-mentality is in most of us very precarious and rarely dominant. The influence of the primitive herd-mentality is generally unconscious, in the sense that the individual himself is unable to recognise that he is being swayed by an obscure craving to conform, and to enforce conformity on others. On occasions of heightened social consciousness, such as political crises, economic crises, crises of class-strife, war scares, and so on, herd-mentality may become dominant, though still in the main unconscious. The individual will accept arguments and valuations simply because they bear the sanction of public opinion, or of the particular group-opinion to which he is loyal; yet he will believe that he has accepted them for reasons of self-interest or for genuinely social reasons.

This picture of the individual's social feeling and behaviour is not complete till we have added a few slight but very important touches of a very different nature, already mentioned in the chapter on Personality. Most individuals do, as we have seen, at times rise to genuine love of some other individual. Most are capable also, to some slight extent, of genuine community behaviour. Important as this is, we must not forget that in the main, however much they conform to the social tradition of altruism, they are at heart individualists. With this qualification always in mind, let us proceed to discuss in more detail the nature of genuine community.

(d) *Genuine Community: Personal Intercourse.*— The word " community " is ambiguous. In the first place it sometimes means a group of individuals, as in the phrase " the Jewish community," and sometimes it means the abstraction or universal character which characterises all concrete communities. In the second place, whether it is used in the concrete or the abstract sense, the word may have either a very general or a more restricted meaning. In the general sense a community is any group of individuals having any kind of social relation to one another. In this sense even the prisoners in a gaol may be said to form a community. But in the more restricted sense, the sense with which we are here concerned, a community is a group of persons who willingly co-operate, who are not merely economically but mentally a source of enrichment to one another, and who prize their social relationship.

Community in this sense must be experienced in the first instance through actual personal intercourse with other individuals in some small group. Larger and yet genuine communities, in which the bond of personal intercourse is absent or fragmentary, may occur; but in these some other kind of bond must form an adequate substitute for personal contact. We will begin by considering only communities based on contact.

The simplest example is a happily married couple. By a happily married couple I mean, not the romantic idealisation of marriage as " two souls in unison," but a partnership in which the very diversity of the members, even if it leads to considerable strain, is on the whole a source of enrichment to both. Larger groups may also in varying degrees fulfil the definition. A family, a school, a college, a religious congregation, a committee, a body of research workers or of any other workers in personal contact, a military unit, a revolutionary " cell," a social club—these and many other kinds of small group *may* be genuine communities. To deserve the name they need not be immune from internal conflict. Indeed the internal conflicts of a community may be one of the main modes by which the members mutually enrich one another. But for the community to be a genuine community, conflict must be subordinate to the common purpose, and must be so regarded by all the members of the community.

I have several times used the phrases " mutual enrichment " and " mental enrichment." Each member of the community is a centre of activity, and in particular of conscious activity, of knowing-feeling-striving. He has his characteristic capacities and needs. The community should enrich him in two manners. In the first place, his intercourse with the other members should enable him the better to fulfil his own personal capacities and satisfy his personal needs. In the second place, friendship with or love of individuals whose character is different from his own should enrich him with experience of the diversity of minds, and should (metaphorically) enlarge his self to embrace other selves of alien type. It is essential to community as a source of mutual enrichment that the members should be different from one another in psychological make-up. A community composed of identical twins living in identical conditions (if this were possible) would be a sterile community. The greater the psychological differences the better, so long as the underlying identity of interest or purpose is strong enough to hold the members together.

In the community of personal contact each member prizes not only the other members as individuals but also the social relationship. In the simplest of all cases the lover loves the beloved, but also he prizes love itself, the reciprocal relationship between himself and the other. Further, while the experience of love affords him a deep sense of personal fulfilment, he will gladly (up to a point) forgo personal fulfilment if thereby he can give greater fulfilment to the other. In the larger community of personal contact a member may sacrifice himself (up to a point) either for the sake of the other members or to preserve the communal relationship.

The common interest or purpose which unites the members of the community may have as its object either the maintenance of the community itself or some goal external to the community. The common purpose of the married couple is chiefly the maintenance of the community itself; though the raising and equipment of children is a purpose which comes under both categories. The common purpose of the revolutionary " cell " is external to itself.

In any actual community, even the most intimate and harmonious, there will be conflicts of personal interests. In so far as the community really *is* a community these conflicts will be willingly subordinated to the common interest. But also, of course, in the best actual human communities, even those based on personal contact, there will be a great deal of sheer individualism. Personal interests, that is, will not always be willingly subordinated, but will sometimes be pursued even to the detriment of the community.

Indeed, genuine community, even by personal contact, is rare and precarious. Some psychologists have claimed that there is no such thing, that the *only* social behaviour is some combination of individualism and instinctive gregariousness, sex and parenthood, conditioned to the stimuli of civilised society. To these psychologists the reply must be that they have overlooked a kind of behaviour which does occur and is essentially different from the other kinds. Rare and precarious as community is, probably most human beings have some slight experience of it. When it has become firmly established in a small group of individuals of fairly high mental calibre it may very thoroughly dominate the behaviour of the whole group.

(e) *Genuine Community : Social Will.*—If it is difficult to achieve community in a small group in personal contact, it is far more difficult, if not impossible, to establish it in a large group, where personal contact cannot bind every member to every other. In the small group the community-mentality is grounded in the fact that the members can realise one another as persons and can respect one another's differences because of the underlying sense of community. In the large community there is no universal mutual awareness.

Something else, however, can in a manner take its place, namely, a firm will for community.

Though the members of a large community may know only a very small minority of their fellows, all are held together in a mesh of social relationships. Directly or indirectly every life is related with every other. Moreover they may have common economic and political interests, common modes of behaviour, common cultural ideals. Up to a point it is possible for each member to realise at least something of the psychological pattern common to all typical members.

This alone would be no sufficient basis for the will for community. But individuals who have also concrete experience of genuine community through personal contact may form an established disposition to behave on the principle that all members of the large group, even though personally unknown to them, are real individuals, with social rights.

This principle is, of course, consciously accepted by the great majority in civilised countries; but unfortunately the fact that it is consciously accepted does not mean that it is necessarily an effective motive in determining conduct. Probably in most acts which seem to spring from the genuine social will the effective though unacknowledged motive is either individualism or herd-mindedness. Most human acts have complex motives. It is often impossible to discover which motive is the decisive motive in forming a decision. Only when there is a clear conflict between the dictates of self-regard and the social will, and the issue is an act of social service, can we be sure that social will really is the effective motive. But such clear conflicts seldom occur. Even the martyr for a social cause *may* be sacrificing himself for the sake of self-esteem. We are entitled, however, to ask how it came about that self-esteem demanded the supreme self-sacrifice. And the answer must be that his ideal of himself was largely determined in the first instance by his recognition of the intrinsic good of community.

(f) *Civilisation.*—If the foregoing analysis is correct,

288

any human society must be thought of as consisting mostly of individuals who are in the main individualistic, though they are constantly and sometimes violently swayed by herd-mindedness, and are to some extent capable of genuine community by personal contact, and to a much slighter extent moved by the abstract social will.

Recognising that this is true of all normal individuals, we may nevertheless classify normal individuals into three grades, namely, those that are on the whole more herd-minded than others, those that are most individualistic, and those that are on the whole more capable of community than others. But we must not forget that every normal individual, no matter what his normal state, may sometimes sink to the lowest or rise to the highest grade of social behaviour.

In addition to the vast majority of normal human beings, who are in the main individualists, we must recognise a smaller class of approximately subnormal or approximately moron rank, whose social behaviour, and indeed all their behaviour, is almost entirely impulsive. They fluctuate between the spasmodic self-assertion of the sub-human animal, spasmodic affection for particular individuals, and spasmodic herd-mindedness.

At the other extreme comes the very small company of supernormals or saints who have brought their whole lives more or less effectively under the control of their will for community. These are so few and so difficult to discover that they should perhaps be omitted from the classification. But on the whole it seems probable that genuine social saints do occur, and that they have sometimes had a great influence.

If society depended solely on the strength of the
genuine social will in men it would be impossible. But
in the main it depends on their self-regarding motives.
It is in the main a system of interdependent self-seekings. No doubt, so long as we are comfortable, we
keep the rules of society largely through sheer easy-
going conformity to tradition, and to some extent
through a very tepid though genuine social will. For,
on the whole, and provided that the cost to himself is
slight, a man would rather behave socially than anti-
socially. But when serious individualistic interests are
at stake he tends either to evade the rules or to keep
them merely for fear of condemnation, while persuading himself that he is really acting from the best
motives.

The scope of the genuinely social will is probably
much less than it is generally thought to be; but it is
not wholly negligible. Both in a comfortable society
and in one that is felt to be in danger of destruction it
does play some part, though in very different manners
in the two cases. In the comfortable and fairly secure
society, in which most of the members are not too fran-
tically struggling to preserve themselves, the social will
does restrain individuals from petty anti-social acts.
It does enable society to function smoothly without
continuous compulsion and espionage. In the hard-
pressed society, for instance in times of revolution, it
may for a while, and precariously, become the effective
motive not merely in a few supernormal individuals
but in large numbers. When this happens, mere herd-
feeling may be drawn in to support it; for those in whom
the social will is but feeble will be induced by mere herd-
feeling to subordinate their self-interest to the common

enterprise of saving or remaking society. But herd-feeling, or herd-mindedness, is a dangerous reinforcement. In times of crisis and of violence it tends to become dominant; while the community-mentality can establish itself firmly only in times of security and peace.

In what we call " civilised society," there is very little that deserves the name. For civilisation, after all, is not a matter of mechanical power and modern conveniences. It is the process of advancing from a less to a more *civil* mode of behaviour. By this I understand the process by which people come to treat one another more civilly, more as *persons*, both in immediate social contacts and in social organisation.

Is man capable of no more truly civilised society than that of our day ? Must the limitations of human nature permanently prevent men from creating a society in which the will for community dominates the herd-mentality and the individualistic mentality, as in our day individualism dominates the others ? Before hastily answering, " No, for human nature cannot be changed," we should remember that, though the will for community is dependent on innate capacities for intelligence and imagination, it is the product of these capacities in relation to the social environment. It is not simply an innate faculty. In general we must recognise that human nature is so fluid that in each generation it can be changed beyond recognition by the impact of the environment. In an appropriate environment, then, there might occur a very much higher degree of the will for community. Let us therefore now try to record the sort of conditions that are required for the existence of genuine community.

IV. PRE-REQUISITES OF GENUINE COMMUNITY

Genuine community, as defined above, entails the distinctively human degree of sensibility toward other individuals and the distinctively human degree of intelligence and imagination. These are presumably rooted in innate capacity, but to repeat, they can be greatly strengthened or weakened by environmental influence.

Genuine community entails also " unity-in-diversity." The greater the mental diversity of the members the better, so long as each can recognise that others, however alien, are sincerely loyal to the common enterprise.

Genuine community entails that the members of the community shall be bound together in mutual enrichment and mutual obligation either by direct personal contact or by the established will for community. It is impossible to have genuine community without a resolute will that all members of the community shall be treated with the respect and kindliness which every individual desires to receive from his neighbours. Personal intercourse and the abstract will for community may be regarded as the two kinds of cement which consolidate communities.

That the members may realise one another's modes of life and thought, their means of communication must be well developed. In the community of contact they must meet and converse and engage in common enterprises. In large communities they must have transport, postal services, journals, radio, and so on, in order that the special needs and characters of particular sub-communities may be to some extent known to all.

On the other hand, the members must not be so cramped by one another's presence that none can properly develop his individuality, assimilate his experience, and retain his personal distinction of character.

That the members may be able to understand and cherish one another they must be nurtured in a common tradition of thought and feeling.

The common culture must be such as to afford a sense that all are united in a common purpose more important than private advancement. The common purpose, as we have seen, may be either intrinsic or extrinsic to the community.

Grave personal frustration is inimical to community. No doubt some degree of struggle and even of defeat is necessary for the health of the individual. The mind that has no difficulties to overcome is likely to be flabby and sterile. The man who knows only personal success lacks depth of experience, and when trouble does arrive is likely to be overwhelmed. Further, the community-will needs to express itself in unselfish devotion to the common task. But sacrifice must be voluntarily incurred, and it must not be such as to lower the individual's mental and moral calibre. Clearly the occurrence of serious and widespread frustration is in itself a violation of community, since the goal of community is the fulfilment of individual capacity. But in another sense also frustration is inimical to community. Individuals of lowly calibre are incapable of true community if they are themselves gravely, continuously and compulsorily frustrated. Exceptional individuals may retain the community mentality in spite of grave personal frustration; but in average individuals frustration soon breeds exasperation, intolerance, vindictiveness, and incapacity for objective thought. In a society in which these mental defects are common, even the unfrustrated members are liable to be infected by the general decay of community. The secret sense of their own un-merited good fortune may drive them to irrational fear and hate of the frustrated.

For practical purposes we may say that there are three main kinds of frustration which tend to make genuine community impossible. They are often closely related. They are: frustration due to untoward per-sonal relationships, economic frustration, and frustra-tion due to the danger of the destruction of the com-munity, for instance in war.

In spite of the important pioneering work of the psychoanalysts, the effects of frustration due to personal relationship are as yet little understood. We are, how-ever, beginning to realise that the relations of children and adolescents to adults and to others of their own age may have grave effects on the development of character. The same is true, though in a less degree, of the relations of adults to one another. Not only sexual disasters, but disastrous relations between master or leader and subordinates may destroy the precarious capacity for community.

But serious economic frustration is at least as harm-ful as any other force inimical to community. Not merely actual hunger but bad home conditions and conditions of work, the constant sense of economic insecurity, the spectacle of the luxury of the more for-tunate, the servility exacted from the wage-slave, mass-produced education, the sense that one's labour is being controlled for the profit of a class rather than for society as a whole, the sense of the futility of the whole economic order of society, the sense that the precious gift of mechanical power is being prostituted for false ends, and above all the sense of personal dereliction and uselessness—all these effects of economic frustration tend to engender in the average individual a state of mind inimical to community.

The third grave source of frustration is the dread of the destruction or serious damage of society, whether by revolt from within or attack from without. Danger is more apt to foster the herd-mentality than the community-mentality. As we have seen, the herd-mentality is essentially a reaction to danger by means of biologically-imposed discipline; while the community-mentality cannot thrive for long without freedom and security. It demands, not uniformity, but diversity, and the realisation of other individuals as intrinsically worthy of regard in spite of their differences from oneself. But in order to resist social danger, from within or without, it is necessary to suppress all those developed activities which are the true purpose of community, so as to concentrate on the single task of defence. The society must therefore be regimented. Personal freedom must be gravely restricted. Eccentricity must be condemned. Criticism of the official policy of defence must be silenced. Free intelligence in general must be bridled or suppressed. Kindliness toward enemies and even toward unfortunate fellow-members is identified with weakness or with treason.

Up to a point all these reactions may be rationally justified as a means of coping with the perilous situation. But instinctive fear and herd-mindedness in response to social danger turn a reasonable tightening up of disci-

pline into an extravagant orgy of repression which tends
to blot out all understanding of what community should
be.

Two other essential pre-requisites of genuine community remain to be stated. Education must be consciously and unfalteringly directed to evoke fully in
all members whatever capacity they have for development in knowing-feeling-striving. Above all, they must
be encouraged to trust their own intelligence, to criticise
even the most sacred beliefs and customs of the community, and to judge all moral issues in the light of their
own well-criticised consciences. Intellectual and moral
integrity must be the supreme goal of education.

The other essential pre-requisite of genuine community is freedom of expression. Communists sometimes argue that complete freedom of expression is impossible and undesirable. No society, they say, will
tolerate or should tolerate the advocacy of policies that
threaten to undermine the basic structure of the society.
To this the answer is simple. Though in societies which
have not attained genuine community some degree of
restriction may be necessary, the fact that restriction
is necessary proves that community has not been
attained. Indeed, the degree of restriction of expression may be taken as a rough measure of a society's
approximation to community. In no existing society
is there complete freedom of expression for all classes.
The Western democracies, bad as they are, are very
superior to some other states in this respect.

V. PROSPECTS OF COMMUNITY

What are the prospects of the development of community in the world as it is in our day? In some

respects they are better than ever before, but in some they are exceptionally bad.

The outstanding increase of the means of communication provides for the first time one essential pre-requisite of world-wide community. Apart from contrary influences, peoples of alien culture can now begin to realise one another as never before. And for good or ill the spread of ideas throughout the world has begun to create a real cosmopolitan culture. If this were to mean the complete standardisation of the cultures of all local societies, it would be a disaster; for community involves diversity. But there is at least a chance that from the present chaos a cultural unity-in-diversity may ultimately arise.

Of common purpose there is as yet but little, since the will for community seldom operates beyond the boundaries of nation or of social class. But the idea of creating an orderly world-community in which national sovereign states shall become mere local governments is at any rate far more familiar than it was before the last European War.

To these favourable influences must be added the fact that unprecedented scientific invention and mechanical power make it possible to organise the world in such a way that every human being might have the opportunity of developing to the full such innate capacity for community as he has.

Unfortunately, these favourable factors are counterbalanced by unfavourable ones. Though there has probably been no considerable change in the incidence of innate social capacity, the new barbarism, now spreading from country to country, the tendency to persecute the free intelligence and the individual conscience, may seriously reduce the proportion of more sensitive and integrated individuals in the world-population. For the present, however, this is not an urgent danger save in the regions controlled by dictators. Even in the small society united by direct personal contact the modern taboo on tenderness has probably rendered genuine community more precarious. By casting doubt on man's capacity for altruism it has tended to weaken the will for community in every sphere.

Frustration of all three kinds mentioned in the preceding section seriously undermines men's social capacity in every country. Frustration from untoward personal relationships may be no commoner than in earlier days; but it is present. And its damaging effect is probably increased by the strain of modern industrial life. The evil effect of economic frustration is increased by the increasing sense that it might be avoided. The sense of danger from attack has increased beyond all expectation.

Unless economic frustration and danger from attack can be removed, the prospects of community, even in the relatively narrow sphere of the national State, are very poor. Of world-community there seems at present little prospect.

Psychologically the national State depends very largely on appeals to herd-mindedness. It is also supported by the community-will of some sections of the population. But in the modern world the community-will cannot logically confine itself within the boundaries of the national State. It must seek world-community or degenerate into herd-mentality in response to danger.

Apart from the grave practical difficulties of organising a world-society, and apart from the formidable pressure of purely individualistic vested interests in the established order, two psychological forces resist the incipient movement toward world-community. The herd-mentality of the nation tends to preserve enmities. The herd-mentality of economic classes, caused of course by real conflicts of economic interest, tends to preserve class-enmities. Until these two great sources of emotional prejudice are overcome there is no hope of genuine world-community.

On the other hand, nothing short of a world-community can satisfy the community-will or afford peace and prosperity to the human race in modern conditions.

Many declare that the ideal of world-community is quite unrealisable. They point out that even on the national scale there is no real community, but only a more or less successful system of interdependent self-seekings, liable at any moment to be swept by waves of herd passion.

True ! Yet if the causes of frustration are abolished, and full use is made of modern communications, and education is consciously, constantly, and whole-heartedly directed toward the creation of responsible world-citizens, even our imperfect human nature might prove capable of world-community. But shall we ever, in our present warped and savage state, even begin to remove the causes of frustration ?

CHAPTER X

SOCIAL CHANGE

I. Some Idealist Theories. II. Economic Determinism.
III. Commentary.

I. SOME IDEALIST THEORIES

(a) *The Problem.*—We have been considering the nature
of community and its present prospects. Clearly the
future of community in the world depends on the
forces, whatever they are, which determine the course
of history. We must now briefly consider some of the
main theories on this subject. Strictly, this is a scientific
rather than a philosophical problem in the narrower
sense. Is it possible by means of careful observation
to form inductive laws descriptive of the course of history ? The subject is so complex that no such scientific
analysis can as yet be made with any accuracy. The
field is therefore left open for speculation based on
very fragmentary and confused evidence. This is not
to say that theories of the determinants of history are
all worthless. On the contrary, as we shall see, at least
one very important principle can be established and
used with great effect, so long as it is not set up as an
all-sufficient principle of explanation.

My reasons for bringing this subject into a book on
philosophy are, first, that when speculation is permis-
sible at all, it should be very strictly criticised from the
philosophical point of view, and second, that, if philosophy is the pursuit of wisdom, philosophers must seek
some understanding of the process of history.

(b) *The Great Men Theory.*—Perhaps the most naive theory of the forces which determine the course of history is that according to which the influence of " great men," of outstanding individuals, is the most significant factor. In this view such famous characters as Alexander, Cæsar, Napoleon, simply through the force of their own temperament and will, simply through their own intrinsic and undetermined spiritual vigour, determine what shall happen throughout vast areas. They impose a particular pattern on events, a pattern of government or conquest or culture. Directly and indirectly they mould the whole future of the race.

Below them, according to the theory, large numbers of minor " great men " have similar but far less important effect. Lower still come the average masses, who are in the main passive to the far-reaching influences of the great.

In its extreme form the theory is too crude to be seriously considered. It overlooks very much that is obvious to any unbiassed student of history. Even the greatest personality must have some raw material through which to express his potency; and the raw material is just the world of physical objects and ordinary people. Obviously this material has a nature of its own, and its effects must not be ignored. It determines the course of history at least as much as the great men. Moreover they themselves are at least in part determined by their social environment and their biological inheritance.

The recognition of this, however, need not blind us to the importance of dominating characters. No doubt circumstances themselves play a great part in making great men what they are. Cromwell, for instance, would never have made history had not the circumstances of his time and place given special opportunity to such a man. But the kind of history that he did make was partly the expression of his own idiosyncrasies. These in turn, no doubt, were in some sense an expression of his environment and his inheritance; but, once in existence, they became a possible important factor in English history. Much good and much harm can be done by leaders.

(c) *Evolutionism.*—Some scientists and philosophers, impressed by human progress and by the evolution of biological species, have conceived that the main force determining the course of history is some kind of teleological drive or Life Force, independent of conscious individual minds but inherent somehow in them, and working through them. This mysterious entity they conceive as striving toward ever more developed consciousness in its races of individuals, creating species after species in age-long experimentation. Similarly in human affairs the Life Force is thought to bud out in a number of races, and to express itself in institutions and cultures, always moving forward (apart from temporary setbacks) to higher social forms and biological forms.

This theory takes us at once into the realm of metaphysics, the attempt to discover by argument the essential nature of reality. We shall later enquire whether metaphysics is a possible study, and whether, if it is possible, Evolutionism is a satisfactory theory. Meanwhile we are concerned only with its relation to history. Do the known facts of history suggest that the course of events has been controlled by a superhuman purposive power or teleological principle?

Many human races have never advanced beyond the primitive level. Many have advanced only to decline. It is true that the more advanced races and societies tend to master the less advanced, but this is more satisfactorily explained in terms of the mere struggle for existence than in terms of an occult teleological drive toward a higher form of civilisation. When we consider the record of human history, do we discover any evidence whatever that cannot be accounted for as a slow and fluctuating progress due to individual intelligence and the effects of a gradual accumulation of wisdom and skill through tradition ?

We must bear in mind also that, though in recent centuries there has been an amazing mechanical and industrial advance, the result may turn out to be not progress but the destruction of civilisation. Does the present situation of the human race strongly suggest guidance by a teleological power ?

(d) *The Hegelian Theory.*—The type of historical theory conceived by Hegel and adopted by most Idealist philosophers is at first sight akin to Evolutionism, because it makes use of the concept of development; but in this theory development does not take place through the operation of purely physical laws, nor through some mysterious teleological Life Force. It is said to be a logical consequence of the character of a changing situation at a given time. The " situation " is not simply environmental. It is the whole situation " man-in-environment." But this, according to Hegel, is to be thought of in terms of mind rather than of matter. Human history is therefore the history of the development of the human spirit; but the human spirit includes its objective world. Thought and reality are one, not two related things. Reality *is* experience. The laws of our thinking are in principle the laws of reality. Human knowledge is reality knowing itself.

Once more we find ourselves faced with metaphysical statements which we will not yet criticise. We will merely consider their application in the Idealist theory of history.

The development of human thought, or the human spirit, takes place, according to Hegel, by a process which he called " dialectical." The condition of culture at any time, he says, contains within itself contradictions; and as the contradictory elements grow in strength the spirit suffers internal conflict, until at last a new condition emerges in which both the conflicting components are transformed and harmonised. The three stages he called respectively " thesis," " antithesis," and " synthesis."

For the understanding of history, then, we must detect in the culture of a people at a given time the conditions in virtue of which that culture must presently be thrown into logical conflict with itself; and we must watch this conflict give birth to a new form of culture in which the conflict is resolved in a new synthesis, a new and relatively stable phase of culture. In this phase too we must seek for a new incipient conflict. And so on.

What is true of the successive phases of a single culture is said by Hegel to be true also of the great sequence of the cultures that have risen and fallen since the beginning of history. The key to the understanding of this process is the principle that the development of the spirit is a dialectical development toward " rational freedom," freedom to will the rational good will. Thus, we are told, in ancient Asiatic culture both law and morality are conceived as external to the individual. He obeys them as the commands of an alien tyrant. Later, in Greece, individuality begins to assert itself. Later still, in the Roman State, sheer individualism is consciously subordinated to the State, which becomes the common end of all individuals. From this condition, in which the individual tends to be overburdened with duties, the spirit rises (we are told) to its full expression of rational freedom in the Germany of Hegel's time.

Thus history is conceived as essentially the consequence of the rational development of the ideas that constitute a culture. Though for Hegel reality and thought are identical, the explanatory concept is the principle of rationality experienced in thinking.

Apart from the question of the scope of the dialectical principle, which I shall discuss more fully at a later stage, the main criticisms to be brought against the Hegelian theory are two. First, it underestimates the fortuitousness and confusion of history. What it describes as a logical development is in fact a bewildering tangle of haphazard influences. Second, it assumes that the governing principle of cultural change is to be found in culture itself, rather than in the environment within which culture is generated. It entirely fails to do justice to the part played by the material world in determining man's actions, institutions, and ideas. It ignores the immensely important geographical and economic influences.

II. ECONOMIC DETERMINISM

We must now consider a very different theory in which the emphasis is laid not on mind but on the material environment. At this point I shall try to give an account of Karl Marx's interpretation of history without discussing the metaphysical aspects of his doctrine. These I shall consider at a later stage. This procedure seems to be justified because Marx's historical theory is in the main independent of the metaphysical theory on which he based it.

It is advisable to say at the outset that I cannot claim to be a thorough student of Marxism, and that what follows was written by one who approached the subject regrettably late in life, and is perhaps unable fully to comprehend it. At least I shall treat it with due respect. And I shall *try* to regard it without prejudice, favourable or unfavourable.

Marx starts by accepting the Hegelian dialectic, but claims to turn it right side up. Human history, for Marx, is not the logical development of thought, changing through a purely ideal necessity. For Marx " the ideal is nothing else than the material world reflected by the human mind, and translated into terms of thought." And Engels declares that " the final causes of all social changes and revolutions are to be sought not in man's brains, not in men's better insight into eternal truth and justice, but in changes in the modes of production and exchange."

We must begin by distinguishing between the two closely associated doctrines which are involved in the Marxian interpretation of history. Economic Determinism is the doctrine that the whole course of history, including the evolution of institutions and ideas, is determined by the impact of the economic environment on man's economic needs. Dialectical Materialism is the doctrine that the course of Economic Determinism takes place according to the dialectical principle. This doctrine has also a metaphysical aspect which we can for the present ignore.

In the true dialectical manner it is conceived that any given stable phase of social development generates within itself its " opposite," and that out of the conflict of the two social tendencies there emerges a synthesis in which what is of permanent value in both appears in a new and harmonious form. A typical example of the dialectical process in history is said to be the growth of capitalism out of feudalism. The feudal system itself generated a bourgeois class that was antithetical to it; for in feudalism every individual was born into a certain social status, whereas the new bourgeois class consisted of individuals who by commercial power were able to break the bonds of feudal status. After a period of conflict a new social order emerged, namely capitalism, in which a new stability was attained. But capitalism itself (we are told) generated the modern proletariat, which is antithetical to it, and must inevitably (we are told) produce a new class-less order, namely Communism.

In the contemporary world a number of dialectical contradictions obviously occur. I cite some examples quoted from Mr. Joseph Needham. Modern capitalistic national States must, for the violent seizure or maintenance of foreign markets, arm their workers; but this is to arm their own potential destroyers. (Perhaps the development of air power has made it unnecessary to arm them, and easy to control them.) Capitalistic States must seek to develop their colonies; but this causes native movements of liberation. Capitalistic States must, to preserve irrational loyalty to themselves, suppress the free intelligence, and substitute for reason some kind of Fascist mythology of race. But to suppress the free intelligence is to suppress the scientists without whose co-operation capitalism cannot function.

It is easy to see that in the very early stages of human social development institutions and ideas would arise as a direct expression of the simple economic life of hunters and fishers, and later of herdsmen and agriculturists. The relations between the individual and the group, the rules of private and public property in instruments and hunting territory and fertile land, and so on, would come into being through the direct pressure of the environment on primitive human needs. Similarly in modern industrial society the ultimate determinant of institutions and ideas is man's contact with the material environment through the immensely complex processes of acquiring raw material and turning it into marketable goods by innumerable industrial techniques. But in this late stage the immediate effect of the environment is complicated by a thousand other influences derived from the past, and ultimately from past environments.

In the earliest stage of social development there would be no class distinctions. But with the change from hunting to pasturage the scope of private property would increase, and consequently there would appear the first cleavage into " haves " and " have-nots." This class distinction would be greatly emphasised by the development of agriculture and property in land. This brings us to the period of recorded history. The landowner's need for cheap labour was satisfied by reducing the less fortunate to serfdom. The whole of subsequent history, according to Economic Determinism, is at bottom an expression of two factors, namely, on the one hand the relation between man and the physical environment which conditions his production, and on the other hand the relation between two antagonistic social classes, namely, the owners of the means of production and the workers, who by one device or another are forced to labour as the owners dictate. The form of this class relationship varies in different ages and localities with the variations of the economic determinants. Thus, by a process of environmental influence which we need not consider in detail, the primitive slave-owning agricultural society develops into the more complex feudal society, and this in turn into the modern capitalistic society. In every case, we are told, the fundamental determinants of institutions and ideas are the relation of man to the material environment, and the relation of the exploiters to the exploited slaves or wage-slaves.

In the archaic slave-owning society and the feudal society the power of the owners is frankly based on physical compulsion; but in the capitalistic society, though it depends ultimately on force, it normally operates through the fact that the bargaining power of the worker in selling his labour is much less than the bargaining power of the master.

Another factor has to be taken into account. Institutions and ideas, once they have come into being, tend to persist long after the situations which created them. Modern capitalist society is shot through and through with vestiges of feudalism, which ceased long ago to have any direct bearing on economic conditions. We retain relics of the old feudal aristocracy, and our moral code is still largely based on ideals suited to feudalism in its prime. At any particular stage of history a struggle is going on between the old customs, which are out of gear with new economic facts, and the influence of the new facts themselves, which tend to produce a new social order, including new institutions, new cultural forms, and a new morality. The more firmly established the old order, the greater the time-lag before the new order can appear; and, moreover, the greater the time-lag, the greater the pent-up pressure that will be generated, and the more catastrophic the change when it does occur. Feudalism gave place to capitalism in a series of minor revolutions spread over a long period. Capitalism, since it is far more highly organised and has far greater resources, and far more effective means of propaganda and repression, and since, moreover, it is a world-wide system, will put up (we are told) a more effective fight and have a more catastrophic end.

Not only do institutions and ideas survive the conditions which produce them, but also, once they have come into existence, they manifest a very vigorous life of their own. They may be handed on from individual to individual and from generation to generation long after they have ceased to be appropriate to anything in the environment. They may become part of the deep-rooted mental habits of the society. Not only so, but also the minds which support them think about them and change them. Their changes consist partly of partial adaptations to changing circumstances; but also they are changed in such reactionary ways as to render them more efficient instruments for the service of the social class which holds them. Thus, for instance, the basic ideas of capitalism come to generate the ideas of

311

Fascism, adapting for capitalism's defence some concepts which were alien to capitalism in its earlier phase. For in its earlier phase capitalism was individualistic. It came into existence through the unfettered economic enterprise of private individuals. But in its later stage, as an established system seeking to defend its declining power, its individualism is modified and subordinated to the " totalitarian " or the " corporate " State.

An important place must also be made in the picture for human individuality itself. Though the theory is a deterministic theory, it does not deny spontaneity to human action. Economic determinism works only because men spontaneously desire certain things. They are not compelled to do so, but observably they do do so. Their behaviour is up to a point predictable. Marxism merely predicts how men in the mass may be expected to act. The environment operates through the needs of human individuals, who are not passive but active. They react to their environment in pursuit of their needs. And though particular individuals may have all sorts of idiosyncrasies of desire, the needs which in the mass and in the long run take effect in determining history are the basic economic needs for food, shelter, security, and comfort. Marxism does not deny that all men have also other needs, some primitive like physical sex, some very sophisticated, like the need for intellectual activity. It does not deny that for the understanding of the behaviour of particular individuals these needs may be very important. It merely claims that when we are dealing with men in the aggregate economic needs alone have to be taken into account.

Marxism need not deny that certain outstanding

individuals may have a disproportionate effect on history, and may complicate the pattern of economic determinism by their idiosyncrasies. But it insists that these great ones are in the main selected by the economic forces which happen to offer scope for just such men. The case of Lenin is an obvious example.

In general, though ideas and institutions and the idiosyncrasies of prominent individuals do play an important part in history, this influence is always subordinate to the primary influence of the exigencies of production and exchange. Whenever a conflict between economic forces and other factors occurs, economic forces must, according to Marxism, in the long run win.

The claim that the movement of culture is determined fundamentally by economic influences and not simply by the spontaneous unfolding of the rational capacity of the human spirit, need not deny that rational thinking does occur and does play an important part. The point is that economic influences themselves select from the innumerable individual thinkings that are going on. People tend in the aggregate to accept just those particular ideas that do accord with the current economic order or with the new order that is struggling into existence. Thus (we are told) the thoughts of Marx and of Lenin are destined to play a great part in future culture just because they accurately reflect the objective facts of capitalist society and the inevitable trend of events in the future.

It is claimed, for instance by Professor Levy, that the degree of development of social life and of culture in any period is limited by the degree of technological development in that period. When the material technique of a society is primitive, conditions of life are penurious. Toil is inescapable. The efflorescence of culture is meagre. Where material technique is well advanced, life, at any rate for the dominant class, is easier and more leisured, and culture blooms more luxuriantly and subtly.

Any social order tends to breed within itself techniques more advanced than those which produced it. When this happens, when a social order has generated a technical power too great for it to assimilate, so that the technique is not allowed to be fully applied for human betterment, then, we are told, the effete order must inevitably be swept away. This happened, for instance, to feudalism, and is beginning to happen to capitalism. The full functioning of scientific technique is incompatible with an order which cannot thrive without a certain scarcity of commodities.

In the Marxian theory the whole of human history, from the primitive phase up to the establishment of Communism in the future, is essentially an expression of class struggle. Class after class fights its way to power, and is in turn overwhelmed by a class rising against it from below. And at every stage the dominant class has wielded a ruthless dictatorship. Formerly, the slave-owning aristocracy, later the feudal aristocracy, to-day the capitalist class, and in the transitional stage toward Communism the victorious proletariat exemplify this principle. Capitalism, we are told, is doomed because the economic structure of the world has already outgrown it, because in new circumstances it can no longer work. It depends on mass-production and expanding markets. In a world overcrowded with capitalist States increasing competition for markets inevitably leads to war and the ruin of the whole capitalist system. In this disorder the proletariat (we are told) will seize power, and after a period of dictatorship by the proletariat a new spirit will come into the world. For the interest of the proletariat is identical with the interest of society as a whole. Consequently this final dictatorship is transitional toward a class-less and truly democratic and communistic society. At last history will no longer be determined by the class struggle, nor will culture be vitiated through and through by the need of the dominant class to distort it as a defence against revolution.

III.   COMMENTARY

It is difficult to discuss any aspect of Marxism without rousing violent emotions. And, when emotions run high, champions on either side tend to make it a point of honour to maintain every tittle of the faith and to destroy heresy root and branch. Yet when we look at the history of human ideas we cannot but be impressed by the fact that even the most significant and potent of them have invariably turned out to be open to serious criticism in one respect or another. Particularly is this true of ideas which have a religious or quasi-religious aspect. And Marxism, mainly because it attacks the established order and the fundamental assumptions of society, is often regarded with religious veneration or religious hate. The fact that Economic Determinism in general and Dialectical Materialism in particular are immensely important principles for the understanding of social change should make us specially careful not to spoil their effect by using them uncritically.

We may, I suggest, unhesitatingly accept the general

principle that in a sense the prime or ultimate determinant of the course of historical events has been the impact of the material environment on man's economic needs. It would indeed be strange if institutions and ideas had adapted themselves as closely as they have done to economic conditions, and yet the real determinants had been something else. The main cause of the common reluctance to accept this theory is probably a vague sense that it is subversive, and a vague repugnance felt against materialism. This last objection we shall not consider till we have opened up the question of metaphysics.

But having granted the general principle that the prime determinant is, or at any rate has been, economic, we must beware of assuming that the dialectical principle, which certainly applies in some striking cases, is always and necessarily the most significant concept for understanding social change.

Without raising the question of the metaphysical validity of the dialectical process, we should note that, if it is to be applied to history, it must not be interpreted too simply. On this point Marx himself insists, but his followers are sometimes less cautious than their master. No doubt the application of the dialectic to history is valid up to a point. In some cases a particular social situation may generate within itself some conflicting factor which may be reasonably regarded as in some respect its opposite or contrary; and the conflict may issue in a new synthesis. But we must not attempt to force the whole of history into one simple pattern. Of course there is a loose sense in which the dialectical principle obviously *must* be universally true. Obviously any social change must spring from some factor which is incompatible with the maintenance of the *status quo*, and may therefore be said to be its opposite. This is merely a platitude. To be significant the principle must mean more than this. It must mean that the original economic situation necessarily breeds its logical contrary, and that out of the conflict of the two there must (apart from external interference) necessarily arise a new social situation, a new system of institutions and culture, which is an improvement on both. It would be rash to assume that such progress is inevitable. The present state of the world, for instance, seems as likely to lead to the destruction of civilisation as to its advancement. The attempt to understand all social change solely in terms of a necessary dialectical principle is likely to lead to a doctrinaire and over-simplified account of history. In fact, even if the dialectical principle is in the loosest sense true universally, it is also too formal and abstract to afford *by itself* a master key to historical problems. Human history is immensely complex. Marxians claim that underlying all this complexity there runs a single theme, upon which the complexity is, so to speak, a mere embroidery wrought by special secondary causes. But when they defend this claim they are compelled to ignore or minimise much that gives each age its concrete and unique character. For instance, they ignore the immense scope of mere chance by which comparatively trivial circumstances can deflect the whole course of history, much as a single stone at a critical point near a stream's source may deflect it to one side rather than the other of a mountain, and perhaps of a continent.

Sometimes, too, they do less than justice to the influence of prominent individuals. It is true, of course, that very often the influence of the " great man " does, as they claim, avail itself of the course of economic determinism. Lenin, for instance, had the intelligence to see which way the economic cat would inevitably jump, sooner or later, if left to itself and the influence of lesser men. He had also the genius and fervour to force it to jump at once with a vigour and precision which otherwise it would have lacked. But " great men " may sometimes retard or even deflect the course of economic determinism. In principle this possibility is allowed by the Marxians. They insist only that in the long run it is the economic factor that counts. This, with some further qualifications that have still to be made, we may admit. For the present I suggest only that, if not Marx himself, then some of his followers are apt to underestimate the length and meandering of that " long run."

One element in the Marxian creed, as we have seen, is the belief that, so long as there is class domination, violent revolution is necessarily involved in the achievement of every new social synthesis. It is involved because the established dominant class will necessarily sit on the safety-valve till the boiler explodes. We may admit that in the present world-situation it is probable that the longed-for synthesis will involve a great deal of violence. It does seem all too likely that, whenever a resolutely progressive party comes into power constitutionally, the reactionary minority will provoke a violent conflict. But it is surely rash to assert that violence must, wherever there is class domination, always and necessarily occur. It is rash to generalise from the course of events in Russia, where the established system was exceptionally inefficient and crudely brutal, and the class cleavage much simpler and sharper than in Western Europe.

Of course there is a sense in which all social change is necessarily " violent," since the established order invariably seeks to maintain itself. But if violence means " bloody revolution," we must insist that no simple generalisation is to be trusted.

The foregoing criticisms are of a minor order. They are only qualifications of the main contention that economic conditions are the prime determinants of history. One more criticism, and a much more radical one, must be cautiously stated. The Marxian claims that in Economic Determinism he has a principle which, properly applied, affords an accurate description of the course of history. To prove his case he has, of course, to *interpret* the facts so as to reveal the underlying economic causes. In many cases the economic interpretation is simple and very plausible, in some cases much more ingenious, and more open to doubt. Clearly it *may* be that in some of these cases some other factor is after all the more significant one, that some other general principle is the key to the problem; and, indeed, that *always* some other principle or principles may interfere with the whole pattern of economic determinism, not very obviously, yet with very far-reaching consequences. Determinism operates through the impact of the environment on human *motives* or needs. It is possible that in certain crucial situations even large masses of men may be actuated by motives which are *not* economic, which are *not* derived from the need for food, comfort, and safety.

For instance, one such motive might be irrational

319

herd-mentality, which by dominating men's behaviour at critical points of history might side-track the simple course of economic determinism. Of course herd-mentality may be regarded as itself an " expression " of economic determinants in the remote pre-human past. The united action of the group was always essential to survival. Thus the environment would tend to evoke whatever latent capacity there was for gregarious behaviour and herd-mentality. But this could not have happened unless in human nature (or animal nature) there had been some potentiality for development in such a manner. Herd-mentality can only occur in creatures that have capacity for *some* kind of mental life. You cannot make a silk purse out of a sow's ear, nor a sow's ear out of sand.

Further, having once come into being, herd-mentality constitutes an independent factor, gravely complicating the course of events. Sometimes it cuts across the dominant, but more recently dominant, individualistic mentality, which responds more systematically to economic considerations. It is possible that the European War, though partly an expression of econo-mic determinism, would never have occurred if the national States had not been able to evoke an immense fervour of pure herd-mentality. It is possible also that subsequent events in Europe have been vastly compli-cated by the same force.

Another independent factor in human nature is the will for genuine community. No doubt it, like all else, has been in a sense evoked by the environment, and may therefore be regarded as an expression of economic determinism. But the environment has *evoked* it; not simply *created* it. Always there must be something upon which the environment works. It may well be that sometimes, for instance in times of revolutionary enthusiasm, such as the first century of Christianity and the Russian Revolution, the will for community has played a crucial part. Possibly neither of these great changes could have been achieved without it. Perhaps it is also destined to play a similar part in a future world-wide revolution in comparison with which the Russian Revolution will seem a crude and rather barbaric first sketch. Subsequently, perhaps, it may sink once more into quiescence. Or, again, perhaps long after that revolution has been accomplished, perhaps after centuries of gradually improving economic and educational conditions, it may become the dominant factor in a more harmoniously developed human nature, and the main determinant of history. Economic Determinism, though perhaps the most useful principle for the interpretation of history during the past and the present, may cease to be the supremely significant principle in the not very remote future, when man (we hope) will have gained far greater facility and power of control over the economic environment.

Religious ideas and habits have, of course, in the past played a great part in determining the course of history. In the Marxian view these are all indirect expressions of the economic environment, working upon the universal human need for food, comfort, and security. I have no doubt that this is largely true. But it is surely unscientific, in the present imperfection of our knowledge of psychology, to declare dogmatically that this is the *whole* truth of the matter. It is at least possible that in the best kind of religious experience there is a core, probably impossible to describe accurately in any human language but none the less actual, which is not derived in this manner, but is a genuine apprehension at the upper limit of human capacity. It is possible that experience of this kind, in outstanding individuals, has played a not inconsiderable part in influencing the conduct of the masses at critical moments of history.

As a matter of fact, the Marxian theory itself has room for all this. For the theory expressly denies *mechanical* determinism. It expressly asserts that qualitatively new factors may emerge in each new synthesis. This leads us to the metaphysical aspect of the theory, which we shall discuss in the course of the next chapter. Meanwhile, it is worth while noting that the more fanatical kind of Marxians often do less than justice to the non-mechanical aspect of their master's thought.

This brings me to the final criticism. The theory that all thought is ultimately an expression of economic influences, though in a sense true, has certain dangerous consequences for Marxism itself. It claims that all thought is to some extent biassed by economic motives. If bourgeois thought is thus biassed, so is proletarian thought, though in a contrary direction. It follows that Marxian theories are open to grave suspicion. Some Marxists admit that proletarian thought *is* biassed, and glory in the fact. For the proletarian bias, they say, is a bias not in favour of a class but in favour of society as a whole. Moreover, no theories, they say, are objectively true in an absolute sense. Theories are true for action. They are true in that action based upon them will succeed. This view, as we have already seen in connection with Pragmatism, leads finally to subjectivism. Marxism is in other respects objectivistic, and in no danger of yielding to subjectivism. But this tendency, not merely to recognise that some degree of bias is inevitable, but actually to glory in it, is extremely dangerous. It encourages some Marxians to dismiss as a mere expression of bourgeois bias any theory which they regard as hostile to Marxism. And for the same reason any theory which these enthusiasts simply fail to understand is likely to be condemned. Even more serious is the danger that the glorification of bias will lead to a gradual abandonment of intellectual honesty and the painfully conceived ideal of dispassionate thought. No doubt it is very difficult to put this ideal in practice, but to reject it as an ideal is to reject civilisation for barbarism.

CHAPTER XI

METAPHYSICS

I. IS METAPHYSICS POSSIBLE ?

(a) *The Meaning of " Metaphysics."*—Several times we have raised issues which have been called metaphysical. It is time to form a clearer idea as to the meaning of " metaphysics," and to enquire whether metaphysics is a possible kind of study or only an impossible dream.

The word " metaphysics " is ambiguous. In the widest of all its possible senses it seems to mean the attempt to discover, by whatever method, the most general or comprehensive principles that are true of the experienced universe, or of everything in the experienced universe, or simply of " reality." A more usual and somewhat more restricted sense is the attempt to discover *by logical analysis of experience* the most general principles that are true of the universe as we experience it. This is what Kant called " immanent metaphysics," in contrast with the still more restricted " transcendent metaphysics." By " transcendent metaphysics " he meant the attempt to discover by reasoning the nature of the reality which was conceived to lie *behind* the world of our ordinary experience. In the following discussion we shall be considering metaphysical theories of various types, but we must always bear in mind Kant's distinction, and his contention that though " immanent metaphysics " was a possible study, " transcendent metaphysics " was logically impossible. There is no need, of course, to suppose that the distinction between the kinds of metaphysics is always easy to apply.

The starting-point of metaphysics in either sense is the desire to construct a comprehensively true description of reality. But " transcendent metaphysics " proceeds on the assumption that, since the experienced world is incoherent and unintelligible, we must suppose it to be in some sense merely an " appearance " of a hidden " reality." The method by which it is hoped to discover reality is rational analysis of the fundamental concepts or categories in terms of which we think about things. Though our perception of reality, and our thought about reality, are confused and self-contradictory, it is supposed that, if only we think hard enough, penetratingly enough, sincerely enough, about the nature of our experience, we may discover some hidden principles in the light of which the whole confusion will be resolved.

Two kinds of fundamental criticism are brought against metaphysics. One is derived from natural science, the other from the logical limitations of our thinking. We will consider them in turn.

(b) *Scientific Positivism.*—The gradual realisation of the immense size, complexity, and subtlety of the physical universe has made it seem unlikely that man should be able to discover anything about the fundamental nature of reality. Man has existed for a very short time. Is it credible that the upstart intelligence of a minute organism should be capable of understanding the essence of everything ? Human intelligence, as we have seen, evolved as a means of mastering practical problems, such as the struggle for food and safety.

Was it likely that this humble instrument could accomplish a task that was profoundly alien to it?

This argument was confirmed by the fact that metaphysics seemed never to make any progress. For many centuries the philosophers had been at work, yet what was there to show for it? There was no agreement among them on metaphysical questions. Science, on the other hand, had moved on from strength to strength. Of course there was plenty of disagreement among scientists; but it was disagreement only along the ever-advancing front of scientific conquest. Behind lay a well-established régime which no one would dream of disputing.

Swayed by such arguments Auguste Comte and others formulated the doctrine of Positivism. All metaphysical problems must be foresworn as beyond the range of human intelligence. The only profitable intellectual task was to pursue the scientific exploration of the world.

(c) *Logical Positivism.*—This sceptical disposition has been outdone by the Logical Positivists. According to them, metaphysics is not merely too *difficult* for the human intellect to tackle profitably; it is *logically* an impossible task. We have several times had occasion to notice this important argument. It is now time to pass our final judgment on it. Mr. A. J. Ayer, in his *Language Truth and Logic*, affirms that, since the metaphysician claims to know by intellectual processes facts that could not be known through sense-experience, and since "no statement which refers to a 'reality' transcending the limits of all possible sense-experience can possibly have any literal significance," all metaphysics must necessarily be nonsense. The fruitlessness of trying by means of logical argument to transcend the limits of all possible sense-experience follows, according to the Logical Positivists, from the nature of the significance of language. The metaphysician, we are told, produces sentences which " fail to conform to the conditions under which alone a sentence can be literally significant." A sentence can only be significant, it is said, if it is verifiable. The only way in which to verify a statement of fact (as distinct from a purely logical, and therefore tautological, statement) is by producing the relevant sense-experience. All statements of fact, if they are to have any meaning, must be verifiable at least *in principle* in sense-experience. Of course it must be admitted that many meaningful statements of fact cannot *actually* be verified in sense-experience, because we cannot put ourselves in the position to have the relevant sense-experience. Of this type is the statement that there are mountains on the other side of the moon. This is not a meaningless statement, because at least we know what *kind* of experience would afford verification of it. On the other hand, in the case of metaphysical statements it is argued that no kind of conceivable sense-experience could possibly, even in theory, afford verification. Therefore all such experiences are meaningless. For instance, the statement that God is an eternal spirit cannot conceivably be verified by any kind of sense-experience, because sense-experience is essentially temporal. It comes into being and then vanishes. Verification of the statement that God is an eternal spirit would have to be given in a sense-experience that was itself eternal. But this is inconceivable to us. Similarly unverifiable and meaningless is the statement that reality, as opposed to mere

328

appearance, is timeless. Other examples are the statements that reality is one substance, or two, or many,
or unknowable.

The Logical Positivist's rejection of metaphysics may
take another form. According to the theory, logical
necessity (as we have already seen) is nothing more than
tautology. Logical argument is mere elucidation of
the content of a definition. It follows that the attempt
to discover an underlying reality simply by deductive
reasoning is futile. No doubt the definitions or concepts which metaphysics analyses are in the first
instance derived from our experience of reality; and,
taken at their face-value, they are approximately true
of experienced reality. But we have no guarantee
whatever that the analysed or deduced content of them
is true *also* of a reality which we cannot experience.

(d) *Criticism of Positivism.*—What is the real value
of these arguments? Let us begin by distinguishing
several kinds of " metaphysical " statements. Some
metaphysical statements of the " immanent " kind really
are *theoretically* verifiable in sense-experience in precisely the same manner as, for example, the statement
that this book was written by a human being. The
statement that there is in the universe " a power that
makes for righteousness " is theoretically verifiable.
If a large number of spectacular miracles were to
occur, all of which obviously produced great good in
the world, we should reasonably regard this as strong
evidence that some superhuman power was interfering
with the natural course of events so as to produce good
results. Logical Positivists might claim that even such
a crop of miracles would not verify the statement about
a benevolent power, but merely the statement that

such events had occurred. This is surely unsatisfactory. If a savage were to hear intelligible speech issuing from a radio loud-speaker, or from a gramophone, he would be justified in inferring that an intelligent being had determined the order of the sounds, in spite of the fact that he could not possibly conceive how the miracle happened or what kind of a being was responsible for it.

Some metaphysical statements, once more of the " immanent kind," though not verifiable in sense, are theoretically verifiable in other kinds of immediate experience. I have argued that moral statements are of this type.

Some metaphysical statements are meaningful but false, because they are demonstrably in conflict with experience. Of this type is the statement that reality is a featureless unity. Whatever reality is, it cannot exclude our ordinary experienced and featureful world.

Some metaphysical statements which are logically incoherent, and therefore in the narrowest sense meaningless, may yet have an important meaning in a broader sense. The statement that God is an eternal spirit or a supratemporal person is self-contradictory because the idea of personality involves the passage of time. In a sense, then, the statement is meaningless. But in another sense it is not meaningless, since we can distinguish between the meaning of " God is a supratemporal person " and " God is a form of physical energy." To this the Logical Positivist replies that these two forms of words are not really *statements* at all. They are made up of meaningful words, and so we can distinguish them; but neither of them as a whole is a meaningful statement. But is this true? We may agree that " God is a form of physical energy " is meaningless, simply because the generally-accepted definition of God logically excludes his being physical energy. But of " God is a supratemporal person " we may perhaps reasonably say that, though it has no *literal* meaning, it has a *metaphorical* meaning, which may be true or false. It amounts to saying " There is something, called God, the definition of which includes the essential characteristics of personality, but also includes an aspect which is not limited by time. We do not know how this can be; but we find in our experience certain facts (say miracles, or inner guidance) which strongly suggest a personal God, and other facts (say mystical intuitions) which strongly suggest that he is not limited by time. It would be more irrational to deny these facts than it is to affirm that God is a supratemporal person." I am not suggesting that this proposition about God is *true*, but merely that it is in an important sense *meaningful*. In general it seems unwise to exclude the possibility of metaphorical meaning.

Perhaps it is worth while pointing out that we sometimes make scientific statements of the same type. " An electron is at once a particle and a train of waves " is a self-contradictory statement, but it may have important metaphorical truth. If a mass of evidence suggests that an identifiable something, called an electron, has certain characteristics of a particle, and another mass of evidence suggests that it has certain characteristics of a wave-train, then a self-contradictory statement which expresses these conflicting facts is not only meaningful but more true than a coherent statement which leaves one or other aspect out of account.

The foregoing analysis suggests that metaphysical statements, to be meaningful, must be at least *partially* (and significantly) verifiable in *some* kind of immediate experience, though not necessarily in sense-experience; and that for literal, but not for metaphorical, meaning they must be logically self-consistent.

Let us now consider the Logical Positivist's other argument against metaphysics, namely, that deduction is merely the analysis of definitions, or concepts, and therefore cannot tell us anything new about reality, or anything about a reality behind experience. If " behind " experience means simply " not experienced, but of the same order as " experienced reality, then the statement denies the possibility of even immanent metaphysics. It is true only in the limited sense that logical analysis of the experienced cannot give us *necessary* truth about the unexperienced. However accurate a concept, however true to the facts of experience, and however accurate our deductive analysis from it, we know of no necessity in virtue of which unexperienced reality *must* conform to the implications of experienced reality. We cannot affirm with assurance that reality *must* be systematic, and that the unexperienced *must* cohere with the experienced. On the other hand, it *may* do so. And if the analysis of a concept *does* suggest that unexperienced reality, *probably*, has certain characteristics, we may reasonably believe that this is the case, until we come across positive evidence that it is not. Reality *may*, after all, not be systematic. Or our analysis *may* have been carried out upon insufficient data. But until evidence refutes it, we may reasonably trust it. The point is that each operation of reason, if it is to be condemned, must be condemned on its own merits, and not on the general principle that *no* analysis of experience can *ever* give us any meaningful information which *could* be true of unexperienced reality.

If, however, " behind " experience means " of an entirely different order from " experienced reality, then it is true that deductive analysis of experienced reality can never give us information about reality " behind " experience. Transcendent metaphysics is impossible. But it is extremely important to realise that we cannot know beforehand where the more modest, immanent kind of metaphysics will lead. In the first place, experience itself is not a fixed thing. What we experience depends largely on our sensitivity and our power of intelligent discrimination. The child's experience, for instance, is different from the adult's, because the adult has learned to detect similarities and differences and other relations which the child overlooks. The advance is made by critical analysis and synthesis which to the child is inconceivable. What is for the adult " immanent " is for the child " transcendent." Similarly, a very much more developed culture than ours would outstrip ours as ours outstrips the child's. Much that in the superior culture was " immanent " would be for us " transcendent," and meaningless. This is an extreme example. The expansion of the frontiers of the " immanent " to embrace what seemed " transcendent " is really happening all the time, little by little, so long as culture does not stagnate.

I suggest, then, that the Logical Positivists have not really succeeded in eliminating metaphysics root and branch, even metaphysics of the " transcendent " kind. But they have certainly done very valuable work in showing the pitfalls and limitations of metaphysics.

For they have at least led us to see that a metaphysical statement, to be meaningful, must be theoretically verifiable either in sense-experience or in some other kind of immediate experience. The only exception to this rule is the case of a metaphorical statement in which, though no single, logically coherent, literal meaning is given, yet two or more conflicting elements *are* theoretically verifiable in some kind of immediate experience.

Unfortunately, even if all metaphysical statements are not necessarily nonsense, we must admit that in practice it is extremely difficult to make any metaphysical statement that has more than a very slight amount of very incoherent meaning. Moreover, of those that have any meaning at all, the great majority must be less true than false. For ever since philosophy began, philosophers have been addicted to making metaphysical statements, and yet they have been unable to come to any agreement.

But metaphysics is not a wholly barren study. If it does nothing more, it at least gives salutary warning against the demonstrable mistakes of the great metaphysicians, and against the much cruder metaphysical statements which are very frequently made by people who do not even know that they are indulging in metaphysics. Logical Positivists might argue that it is enough to recognise the logical impossibility of metaphysics, without wading through floods of meaningless verbiage. But this argument is too facile. We must arm ourselves by examining some of the main types of metaphysical theories. In doing so we may perhaps gain something more than mere scepticism about metaphysics. We may end by saying, " Though none of these theories is a true account of reality, all probably contain some slight elements of distorted truth; and reality itself, whatever it is, is at least as rich and subtle as these theories."

I propose, therefore, to devote the rest of this chapter to tracing the main stream of metaphysical thought through Descartes, Spinoza, Leibniz, Kant, Hegel, Marx, Bergson, the Vitalists, the believers in " Emergence," and Whitehead.

II.   PARITY OF MIND AND MATTER

(a) *Descartes*, a devout Christian, living in the early days of modern science, and himself a pioneer of scientific experiment and theory, was torn between faith and scientific curiosity.   He determined to seek intellectual justification for the orthodox religious beliefs which were already being attacked on every side by the increasingly confident materialists.   He supposed himself to be converting the infidel by reason.   " I desire no one," he declared, " to believe anything I have said unless he is constrained to admit it by force and evidence of reason."

Seeking a touchstone by which to test all ideas, Descartes resolved never to accept anything for true which he did not " clearly know to be such."   But he needed some principle by which to judge whether statements were true and certain.   Such a principle he supposed himself to have discovered in the formula that only beliefs which we " clearly and distinctly conceive " are true.   The test of truth was not correspondence with sense-experience but consistency of conception.

Bearing this principle in mind, Descartes scrutinised

his whole experience and came to the conclusion that he could doubt almost everything, including sense-experience; but that one thing at least it was impossible to doubt, namely, his own existence as a thinking being; for, in the very act of doubting, he was thinking. " I think, therefore I am."

It seemed to Descartes that in formulating this proposition he had discovered a truth which was indubitable, and might be used as the foundation of all philosophy. But he was mistaken. He unconsciously assumed that thinking must be the act of something other than itself, namely a thinker. This assumption may be true, but it is certainly open to question. Strictly the starting-point of his argument should have been merely " Thinking is happening." From this it is not possible to infer " Therefore I am." Descartes, however, believed that at one stroke he had established the reality of a mental or spiritual substance whose whole essence and nature consisted only in thinking. It was a substance without place, independent of all material things, wholly distinct from the body, and more easily known than the body. Moreover, he believed, it would exist even if there were no body. This conviction of the self's immortality was, of course, ingrained in him from childhood by orthodox teaching, and it was natural for him to suppose that it was implied in the very nature of a thinking being.

Descartes believed that he could pass logically from the reality of the self to the most remote metaphysical truths. Thus, because he was not merely a thinking but a desiring being, he was not wholly perfect, not wholly complete; since to desire is to desire something which is lacked. But if he was an imperfect being, how came it that he was able to *conceive* a perfect being, namely God? Surely, he argued, he must hold this notion from some nature which in reality was more perfect than himself. For it was impossible to have an idea which was not in the first instance derived from reality, however much it was distorted by the thinker. And the idea of perfection seemed to Descartes an absolute quality which *could not* be the result of distortion. " I should not have the idea of an infinite substance, seeing I am a finite being, unless it were given me by some substance in reality infinite." Descartes concluded that his idea of God as a perfect being proved that such a being existed.

The answer to this famous argument, as we have already seen, is that perfection is no such absolute quality but a mere abstraction from the imperfect objects of experience. A perfect circle is one in which no flaws can be detected. A perfect man is a monster in whom all virtues are unlimited and no vices occur.

Applying his principle of clear conception to his experience of the external world, Descartes thought that he conceived clearly what we call space. It was that which was indefinitely extended, and divisible into figures. Sensory qualities, however, he regarded as confused images, fictions of the mind. Not these qualities, but merely shape, might be allowed to matter.

But he notes a difficulty. Though only what can be clearly conceived can be *true*, it does not follow that whatever can be clearly conceived *exists*. In the case of God, the perfect being, " existence is comprised in the idea " of it; for if it lacked existence, this lack would constitute an imperfection. (Descartes failed to see that even if the *idea* of a perfect being includes the

337

idea of existence, this does not prove that such a being exists.) Up to this point Descartes had satisfied himself that extended matter *might* exist (since it could be clearly conceived), but he had no proof that it *did* exist. But the belief in the existence of God enabled him to give an ingenious proof of the existence of matter. Obviously the senses may mislead. Dreams and illusions force us to admit this. Clearly conceived extension, including figure and number, seemed to Descartes indubitable; yet even figure and number may deceive, since they also may occur in illusion and dream. He had therefore to face the possibility that God had given him false intuitions, both of sense and of reason. But no; this, he argued, could not be. God, the perfect being, must be good, and therefore would not so grossly deceive. But, again, what if not God but a malignant demon had given these intuitions, purposely to deceive? Surely, Descartes protested, a perfect God would not permit any demon to perpetrate so great a deception as this.

Thus Descartes established the existence of a material world, and felt himself entitled to formulate his dualism of thought and extension, or mind and matter. His theory was, of course, a philosophical version of the vague dualism of common sense, and it has haunted philosophy ever since.

Having declared that mind and matter were two distinct substances, he was faced with the problem of explaining their relation. The most intimate of all extended objects, and the one through which alone he had intercourse with the rest of the physical world and with other thinking beings, was, of course, his own body. What, then, was the relation of the thinker or soul to his body ?   Anatomical research led Descartes to believe that the " seat of the soul " was the pineal gland, a small organ in the centre of the brain, recently ascertained to be an atrophied third eye.   He supposed that from this central position the soul somehow controlled the " animal spirit," which he conceived as an extremely subtle medium between mind and matter, permeating the whole body.   This attempt to introduce a link between body and mind, far from solving the problem, merely doubles it, since it becomes necessary to explain the relation between the link and each of the two substances.

There was another aspect of the problem, already noticed in an early chapter.   Descartes was a pioneer of the idea of physical mechanism.   Material substances were supposed to interact with one another according to strict mechanical law.   How, then, *could* the soul influence the body without interfering with the determined course of physical events ?   It was necessary to suppose that the soul in effect created or annihilated physical energy in order to interfere.

Descartes' failure to give a satisfactory account of the relation of the two substances, matter and mind, led many subsequent philosophers to reject dualism.   They were then faced with three possibilities.   Spinoza preserved the parity of mind and matter by denying them rank as substances and regarding them as two attributes of the one real substance.   Idealist philosophers denied the reality of matter, and declared either that minds were substances (Leibniz) or that the only substance was the one Absolute Spirit (Hegel).   Materialists regarded matter alone as substantial.

(b) *Spinoza* was a man of very different temper from

Descartes. He had no desire to defend orthodoxy or to compromise with it. He was a Jew who had been excommunicated from the Synagogue on account of his beliefs. His work is inspired by a combination of intense intellectualism and intense religious feeling of a kind which was far from acceptable to the established religions. He came to be regarded as the arch-atheist; yet a later writer called him the " God-intoxicated " philosopher. It is important to realise that whatever Spinoza's intellectual errors, he did live according to his theories. Though his philosophy was at bottom in a sense egoistic, his personal conduct was unostentatiously but sometimes heroically generous. For in practice he behaved as his philosophy dictated, namely, to embrace all men's needs within the scope of his egoism. In another respect also he lived his philosophy. He was true to the philosophic spirit. His whole life was dominated by the peace of mind which he called " the intellectual love of God."

The motive of Spinoza's philosophical venture was the search for some permanent and perfect object of devotion. He longed to know " whether in fact there might be anything of which the discovery and attainment would enable me to enjoy continuous, supreme, and unending happiness." What ordinarily passed for happiness depended on precarious objects, and was itself precarious. He determined to anchor his own happiness to something eternal and infinite.

The philosophy which resulted from this motive is one which is dominated by the idea of an eternal and perfect substance. It does less than justice to finite things, which he regarded as incompletely real. Even the best of them, he felt, were not worth desiring.

He rejected Descartes' theory that mind and matter are distinct substances. A substance, he said, is that " the conception of which does not need to be formed from the conception of any other thing." In his view there can only be one substance, namely, the whole universe, or what he calls " God or Nature." This one substance must have an infinite number of attributes. An attribute is " that which the understanding perceives as constituting the essence of a substance." Spinoza believed that all attributes must in theory be logically deducible from the nature of the one substance. (Of course he could not demonstrate that this was so.) Only two of the infinite attributes, according to Spinoza, are known to us, namely " thought and extension," or mind and matter. All particular minds and particular physical things are said to be " modes " of substance. A mode is " that which is, and is conceived by means of, something else." A particular mind is a mode of the thought-attribute of the one substance; a physical thing is a mode of the extension-attribute. No particular mind or physical thing is a self-complete reality. It is merely a particular manifestation or quality of the one substance.

All our thoughts, all our experiences, are experiences within the universal experience which is the thought-attribute of the one substance, " God or Nature." What a man knows of the physical universe is an excerpt from the perfect universal understanding. Moreover, a " mode " of extension (a physical object) and the idea of it are one and the same thing, expressed in two ways. Things and our experiences of them are not distinct entities. The physical universe is simply the material aspect of the perfect universal understanding; and this in turn is the thought-aspect of the physical universe.

This principle enabled Spinoza to explain the relation of body and mind. Rejecting Descartes' theory of the interaction of two substances, he accepts a kind of parallelism or double-aspect theory. Thought and extension has each its own system of necessary laws. In matter everything is determined by physical laws, in mind by mental laws. But since thought is merely the thought-aspect of matter, and matter the physical aspect of mind, there is an exact correspondence between the two.

Spinoza conceived the universal experience in a very intellectualistic manner. In his view it is all-comprehensive knowledge, but it is without any purpose which can be regarded as the purpose of the universal mind itself. Purpose implies lack, and the universal mind is complete, perfect. Though it has no purpose of its own, it embraces all purposes, and both sides of all conflicts. We, with our conflicting desires, are all members in the infinite understanding which is God. Our thoughts, taken in isolation from the rest of the universal experience, are one and all incomplete, and therefore false; but taken in their proper place in the universal experience, or in God's thinking, they are factors in truth.

This view of the individual and his errors is very unsatisfactory. If a finite mind is really no more than a strand of thought in the infinite mind, how comes it that it can be in error at all ? How can our thoughts be for us *other* than they are for God ? How do our experiences come to be used twice, so to speak : once truly in the universal understanding of God, and once erroneously in our own finite understanding ? To be in error, the mind must have a finite individuality of its own, isolated from the thought of God. Mere qualities cannot make mistakes.

Nor can they have emotions and desires. According to Spinoza, our emotions are simply ideas of the " effort " of a particular physical body, the effort by which it maintains its separate existence. Every finite thing has an inherent tendency to preserve its unity and equilibrium in spite of the influences of other things. This is the source of our self-conscious self-regard. Indeed, it is the source of all our actions. We are essentially egoists. All finite minds have these separatistic emotions. All seek the petty, partial ends which appear desirable to their finite, blinkered nature. Good and bad are wholly relative to our finite nature. They are subjective. In the divine understanding they are regarded with complete detachment. Nevertheless, there is one reasonable goal of a man's endeavour, namely participation in the divine understanding, the acceptance of the universal view, in which all goods and evils are transcended. The goodness of this is subjective, of course, since it depends on the man's own lack of that perfection; but it is nevertheless the reasonable goal for him, since it constitutes the fulfilment or perfection of his imperfect nature. To some extent all of us can strive to transcend our limitations and enter into the full understanding which is God; who contemplates all existence truly and without emotion, though with the beatitude that belongs to perfection. For our finite minds salvation lies in learning to detach our interest from all petty ends and seek only the " intellectual love of God," which consists of tranquil acceptance of the universe as it really is. This intellectual love of God, to which we should all strive if we would attain secure and lasting happiness, is at once our love of God and God's love of himself; and also his love of us, who are modes of himself. When a finite mind achieves this consummation, it simply enters into the perfect understanding, the experience in which " God or Nature " contemplates itself. In the intellectual love of God we do not love something *other* than ourselves, for we are not distinct from God.

Sin, in this view, is of the same order as error. It is the willing of a merely partial good at the expense of other goods, which equally deserve to be taken into account. It is enslavement to the passions natural to the separate, finite creature; and it is neglect of the perfect whole.

Since in Spinoza's view we are all essentially egoists, sin consists in seeking a minor or fleeting kind of self-fulfilment at the expense of a major or more enduring kind. The only fully satisfying life is that which is dominated by the intellectual love of God, and is not side-tracked by the passions. The " passions " include spontaneous pity and charity. We must do good acts *not* for pity but because they are rational. Pity is mere weakness; and weakness, no matter how amiable, is a vice. So is ignorance. Sin is devotion to a minor good in *ignorance* of a greater good. For in Spinoza's view, if we really *know* the good, we cannot but will it. This is unsatisfactory. By sin we *mean* essentially something more than this. We mean willing what is *known* to be evil. Spinoza's theory of sin is also open to a criticism of the same kind as that which we brought against his theory of error. *How comes it* that mere qualities of the one substance can have wills of their own, and sinful wills ?

In the orthodox view sin is thought to involve freedom. In sinning we *could* do otherwise than we actually do. For Spinoza, however, all our acts are determined; since they are the outcome of the laws of matter and mind. But though he allows no possibility of arbitrary choice, he offers what he regards as the only kind of freedom that is worth having; not freedom to struggle against destiny, but the freedom which consists in knowing the truth and accepting it with peace of heart in the intellectual love of God.

The temper of our own age is out of tune with the temper of Spinoza. For most of us it is easier to see the faults than the merits of his philosophy. We readily condemn it, not only on account of its many inconsistencies, but also because it stresses the whole at the expense of the parts, and because it disparages the values of ordinary life, advocating an inhuman detachment. We incline to regard the hunger for an all-embracing or ultimate reality as merely a flight from immediate reality with all its urgent claims.

Undoubtedly Spinoza was so obsessed by wholeness and infinity that he entirely failed to provide a satisfactory status for particular things and minds. But to charge him with flight from reality seems ludicrously unjustified. The charge is refuted by his personal life. On one occasion when he was in a friend's house, his enemies incited a mob to clamour at the door for his life. Rather than embroil his friend by remaining in safety, he faced the crowd. By reasonable speech he persuaded them to disband. Indeed, Spinoza may be regarded as the outstanding example of the true philosophic temper which combines courageous but reasonable action with unshakable detachment and peace of mind.

Though intellectually Spinoza's philosophy should perhaps be regarded as a splendid and immensely significant failure, the fact that it was a failure must be attributed, I believe, partly to the fact that he was preeminently conscious of two seemingly incompatible aspects of experience, both of which may be called religious. One is the intuitive and non-rational perception of the beauty or rightness of the experienced universe as a whole. The other is the intuitive and non-rational devotion toward the human enterprise within the universe. Intellectually he failed to reconcile these two experiences, but he lived in loyalty to both.

In our age we need, I believe, not less but more of the spirit of Spinoza. We are being submerged in a great wave of irrationalism, in a cult of unreason, of impulse, of animality, of savagery. All this originated in a wholesome reaction against the complacent intellectualism of an earlier age; but it has become extravagant, and is dragging us into barbarism.

III. IDEALISM

(a) *Essentials of Metaphysical Idealism.*—We have been considering theories in which mind and matter are given equal status, either as distinct substances or as attributes of a single substance. We must now turn to theories in which mind is taken to be the more significant concept for understanding reality.

In an earlier chapter we discussed Epistemological

Idealism, or Idealism as a theory of knowledge. We now turn to Metaphysical Idealism, or Idealism as a theory of the fundamental nature of reality.

Metaphysical Idealism may be said to begin with Plato. As we have already seen in connection with ethics, Plato held that the universal " ideas " or forms to which particular things approximate were more " real " than the particular things themselves. According to him, manhood is more real than men. He did not, of course, conceive of the forms as merely subjective ideas in our minds. They were objective to us. All the same, in the Platonic theory the world of universal forms, which was the reality behind appearances, was evidently in some sense a spiritual reality. The supreme form was the form of the Good. Plato did not distinguish as sharply as we do between the mental and the non-mental; but his theory that the universal forms, or characters, or " ideas," or (as some would say) concepts, were more real than particular things was certainly the germ from which, centuries later, sprang modern Absolute Idealism.

In considering modern Idealism, we must notice two types of theory, namely, pluralistic and monistic. The first, revolting against Spinoza's monism, postulates an infinite number of individual mental substances, the finite minds. The other, deeply impressed by Spinoza's monism, asserts that the whole universe is a single mind, and a single substance. Both agree that matter is merely an " appearance," with no existence apart from the minds (or mind) in which it is conceived.

(b) *Leibniz* was a courtier and a man of affairs who devoted only part of his energy to philosophy. He had a legal training, and as well as being a great philosopher he was a great mathematician. He invented the differential calculus. Like Descartes, he was anxious to show his agreement with orthodoxy, and for this reason was unwilling to acknowledge his debt to Spinoza.

Leibniz's philosophical aim was to preserve the individuality of human minds while giving a satisfactory account of their inter-relatedness. He also sought to do justice to the part played by purpose in the universe. His philosophy is often regarded as at once arid and fantastic, but to the philosophic mind it affords a very interesting and fertile study. It is a remarkable product of intellectual acuity conflicting with subservience to orthodoxy. And it contains the germs of many modern ideas.

Like Descartes and Spinoza, he worked with the concept of substance and attribute. But he defined a substance as that which persists. through change. Attributes might change, but not the substance itself. According to his theory, the change of the attributes of a substance, or the development of a substance, is never caused by the influence of anything external to the substance. All its changes are consequences of the nature of the substance itself. This theory, that substances could not in any way affect one another, was a consequence of Leibniz's insistence on the reality of finite individuals. If an individual is completely real, it must in his view be completely independent of external influences. If intercourse of any kind whatever is allowed, the theory that an individual is a self-complete substance must be abandoned.

Leibniz insists that substances are active; but the activity of a substance, he says, affects only the future states of the substance itself. Each substance is a world to itself, and an ever-developing world.

Obviously this theory that individuals are completely isolated substances is very unplausible, since individuals *seem* to be in constant interaction. This difficulty Leibniz solved by a very ingenious device, namely, his theory of " pre-established harmony." His substances, it will be remembered, are all mental. He calls them " monads." They are infinite in number. No two of them are exactly alike. Each unique monad is a completely isolated and ever-changing world of experience; but although the changes within each monad happen solely by the necessity of its own nature, yet all changes, says Leibniz, happen *as if* they were due to the effects of other monads. Thus in a manner each monad " mirrors " the rest of the universe from its own particular point of view. This, then, is Leibniz's famous theory of "pre-established harmony." In the beginning God, the supreme and uncreated monad, so fashioned the infinite host of created monads that of their own nature they must evolve in this manner. He made them to be like a number of musicians who, though out of hearing of each other, play in perfect co-ordination because they all began playing their assigned parts together at a common signal and at the same tempo.

Though the monads are all mental, they are of many ranks, ranging from completely unconscious mental activity to clear intellection far beyond human power. Roughly there are three kinds of monads. Lowliest are the " bare monads," which, though mental beings, are unconscious. The notion of unconscious mentality is far from clear. Apparently it means that consciousness in these cases is too faint or too confused to be noticed. The " bare monads " are centres of mere appetite and aversion. They are without memory. Next in rank are the " souls," which are conscious in the animal manner. They have memory, feeling, attention, but are neither rational nor moral. Finally come the " spirits," or human souls, which are more clearly conscious; and, moreover, are self-conscious, and also rational, and morally sensitive and responsible. All monads are eternal; but only spirits have true immortality, since they alone have continuity of experience beyond this life.

Since all substances are mental, material things are not substances. Matter is simply the " appearance " of substances of various kinds to one another. Not that the " appearance " is direct; for this would mean that substances influenced one another. It is merely an " as if " kind of appearance, resulting from the pre-established harmony. Further, matter is essentially, not extension, but resistance, hardness; or rather the apparition of resistance in the completely isolated life of human minds. The ultimate units of matter are not atoms (or electrons, etc.) but monads, lowly minds. Matter is the " appearance " of innumerable unextended centres of spiritual activity. It is an " appearance " in human minds, and through pre-established harmony.

If minds alone are substances, what sort of thing is a human body ? It is the " appearance " (to oneself and to others) of a vast group of monads of different ranks, mostly of the order of " bare monads." These are subordinated to several " souls," which are in turn subordinated to the " spirit " which is the self or " I " of the man. Every one of these monads, of course, fulfils its own destiny by internal necessity; but the changes of all are related by " pre-established harmony." In the lower monads, however, changes are sometimes to be accounted for by reference to changes in higher monads. That is, in some cases God made the lower such that they must spontaneously behave as they do *because* he wanted them to have a certain relation to the higher, through the system of pre-established harmony. Thus, although there is no interaction between the spirit of the man and the monads which appear as his body, in a sense the final cause or reason for what happens in the body monads is to be found in the spirit of the man.

In the experience of every monad there occur changes in clarity of perception. In the case of human spirits there is normally an advance in clarity from infancy to maturity. All monads strive for greater clarity; that is, toward greater " magnitude of positive reality," greater spiritual perfection. Goodness and reality of mental being are either identified or very closely related. " Pleasure " is how we feel when we attain greater perfection. Reason should lead us to seek complete and lasting felicity, but unfortunately by instinct we tend toward merely partial and fleeting fulfilments.

Leibniz's theory of pre-established harmony involves determinism; but as an orthodox Christian he clings to free will. All monads, he insists, act spontaneously, according to their own inherent nature. Their behaviour is contingent, not logically necessary. But the monads of lower order are coerced by the passions, by the insistence of immediate ends; while the spirits, with their greater clarity, can emancipate themselves from their passions for the sake of the ideal of spiritual perfection, or greatest possible "magnitude of positive reality." In Leibniz's theory every act of a monad follows necessarily from its preceding state. All its behaviour is necessarily implied in the nature that God originally gave it. Leibniz does his best to explain away this determinism, since it conflicts with religious orthodoxy. For orthodoxy, sin must be positive. It must not be mere ignorance, mere lack of knowledge. Merely seeing the good must *not* necessarily lead to choosing it. The monads must be in some sense free to do or not do what they know to be good. Leibniz therefore insists that, though all the acts of a monad are determined, and in theory predictable, yet also they are free. God made them such that they would *freely* act in determinate manners in accordance with pre-established harmony.

God's primordial aim in creating, Leibniz says, was to produce as great perfection as possible, to create "the best of all possible worlds." Evil springs not from God's will but from eternal truths which are independent of his will. The best of all possible worlds must contain some evil. Though the perfection of a monad consists in its attainment of perfect clarity, and all spirits are destined finally to reach perfection, it is necessary for the perfection of *the world* that all should start as bare monads and pass upwards through æons of striving: spirits alone among monads are ends in themselves. Other monads are for the sake of spirits, or for the sake of the perfection of the world. God's aim is single, but it has two complementary aspects, namely, the perfection of the world and the perfection of individual spirits, or the creation of the company of the blessed, which he calls " the City of God." These two aspects support each other through pre-established harmony.

The main criticism to be made against Leibniz is the opposite of the main criticism of Spinoza. Just as Spinoza sacrificed individuality to the unity of the whole, so Leibniz sacrificed the whole to individuality. The theory of pre-established harmony is a heroic effort to do justice to the unity of the whole without infringing the substantiality of individuals; but it is unsupported by any evidence. Moreover, the insistence on the plurality of self-complete substances leads straight to solipsism. For if the substances are wholly unaffected by one another, no one of them has any adequate reason to postulate the existence of others.

But though Leibniz's theory may be regarded as a *reductio ad absurdum*, it is well worth study, not only as a brilliant intellectual achievement, but also because, like Spinoza's theory, it contains many ideas which have played an important part in the subsequent history of thought.

(c) *Absolute Idealism.*—Having considered the outstanding example of Idealistic Pluralism, we must turn to Idealistic Monism, or Absolute Idealism, in which individual minds are regarded as mere excerpts from the one reality, which is the absolute spirit.

After Leibniz, leadership in philosophy passed for a while to Britain, and its main theme was not metaphysics but the theory of knowledge. We have already traced that movement through the thought of Locke and Berkeley to its culmination in Hume's phenomenalism. In this view, as we have seen, reality consists wholly of the stream of immediate experience. Any attempt to discover any ulterior, metaphysical reality is doomed to failure.

Hume's great critic, Kant, agreed that metaphysical knowledge, at least of the kind that he called transcendent, was impossible. Behind the world of mere appearances, which Hume tended to regard as the sole reality, Kant, as we have seen, set an entirely unknowable reality or thing-in-itself. All the perceived and conceived characters of experience, in his view, are created by the mind in response to stimulation by the unknowable reality. Thus thoughts do not, as is generally supposed, conform to things; on the contrary things-known must conform to the inherent categories of the mind, to our innate principles of sensibility and understanding. This was Kant's famous " Copernican Revolution " in philosophy. Even time and space must be regarded as mere appearances, due to the limitations of our sensibility. Reality itself must not be thought to be either spatial or temporal. Similarly when we look inward, we find, according to Kant, not the soul but merely " internal phenomena." Whether behind these there is a particular individual spirit or the identical universal spirit we cannot know.

As we have seen, Kant pointed out that the mind was not (as Hume had said) a mere sequence of " impressions " and " ideas," each independent of the rest. Each element in experience was intrinsically related to all others. Everything was what it was in virtue of its relation to other things. This insistence on the unity of experience and the intrinsic relations of its parts was the starting-point of Absolute Idealism.

Though Kant was an idealist, in that he regarded thought as a more significant concept than matter, he was not simply a subjective idealist. In his works there are two tendencies—one subjectivist, the other objectivist. The world of appearances, though inherently logical, and therefore in Kant's view mental, in structure, is objective to the individual mind. In principle, and apart from private errors, the same world of appearances is common to all men. For the general structure of the world of appearances is created not by individual idiosyncrasies but by the fundamental capacities or categories common to all human minds. We are therefore not imprisoned from one another in distinct solipsistic universes.

In Hegel's philosophy the objectivist tendency in Kant is emphasised. A completely unknowable reality, he says, is a completely unnecessary fiction. In principle reality must be knowable. In fact, in principle reality *is knowledge*; not, of course, simply the knowledge of finite minds, but all-comprehensive knowledge. According to Kant, reality is featureless, because to assign it any features would be to deprive it of other features, and it must be infinite. But, according to Hegel, such a reality would be simply nothing at all. Reality, in his view, is a systematic, rational structure, continuous with the world as known in human experience.

And from the point of view of the individual experience reality is objective. It is what it is, no matter what the individual believes it to be. Nevertheless, in principle, thought and reality are identical. The individual human mind is an excerpt from the more comprehensive mind which is society, or society's knowledge; and this again is an excerpt from the mind which is the universal spirit. The structure of the individual human mind is logical throughout. So is his mental development from birth to maturity. So is the social mind, and the development of society. Continuous with this again, and essentially logical, is the structure of the universe as a developing process, and also the structure of the eternal Absolute Spirit *within* which the temporal process is in some sense an eternal factor.

In our day it is difficult to accept Hegel's faith in the ultimate logicality of the universe. We have grown sceptical. We can discover no necessity in virtue of which the universe *must* be systematic through and through. Even if it is, we can no longer believe that it must therefore be essentially " idea." *If* the objective world is logical in structure, its logicality is its own, and we have no reason to call it mental.

According to Hegel, human self-consciousness is in an important respect a microcosm of the all-inclusive reality, the Absolute. For reality is not simply object or simply subject. It is at once knowing and known; just as, in human self-consciousness, the self is at once knowing and known. The Absolute consists at once of the total reality, which we know partially as the multifarious universe, *and* of the true knowing of all this together in the single universal self-consciousness.

One may " feel it in one's bones " that in some sense the Whole is, indeed, self-conscious; and yet one may fail to be impressed by the rational processes by which Hegel and his followers claim to demonstrate this conclusion. No wonder that such daring flights of reason have frightened so many cautious minds, and driven them into Positivism.

We have already seen that for Absolute Idealists only the Whole is fully real. Each particular fact is fully constituted by its intrinsic relations within the whole system; and so, taken by itself, it is a mere abstraction. We must certainly admit that *our knowledge* of any thing is constituted by our knowledge of its relations to other things. We cannot *know* the red of a rose save in contrast with other colours. But for Hegel, since knowledge and reality are identical, the rose *itself* is constituted by its relations to the rest of the universe, its relations of likeness and difference, position, causation, and so on.

Between extreme Monists and extreme Pluralists there is a deep difference of temperament or taste. Perhaps no reconciliation is possible. But the mind that has no extravagant leaning in either direction can see the weakness of both extremes. In respect of the essentially monistic theory of internal relations it is clear that if each thing is *wholly* constituted by its relations to other things, if A *is* its relations to B, and B *is* its relations to A, there is nothing left to have the relations, nothing but the omnipresent and characterless Absolute, which in its characterlessness is reduced to sheer nonentity. On the other hand, if we insist on the complete independent reality of particular things, we incur all the difficulties of Leibniz. Somehow, even at the cost of failing to find a satisfactory theory, we must insist on the co-equal reality of parts and whole, and of terms and relations within the whole. We must be content to say " In a sense things are constituted by their relations within the whole; but in another sense the whole is constituted by its elements in relation."

For the Absolutists true wholes are always more " real " than their parts. They regard the concept of " organism " as all-important. The Absolute is organic. There is certainly a sense in which a living organism is more of a whole than a mere aggregate, like a heap of stones. We are tempted to say that it includes something more than the atoms that compose it, namely, the form or pattern which determines the arrangement of its atoms. Its form in immaturity, moreover, is to be understood only by reference to its mature form. It is a whole both in space and in time. Is the universe, the whole of being, organic in this sense ? Perhaps it is, but we have little or no evidence on the subject. And the attempt to demonstrate by reason that it must necessarily be so is doomed to failure, since there is no necessity that the universe should be rational.

This extreme monism seems to be based on a confusion of " real " and " true." Doubtless you cannot say the whole *truth* about a particular thing without saying the whole truth about the whole universe; but the particular thing is no less *real* than the whole universe. Particular things just *are*, and so is the whole universe.

In the Hegelian system time (like space) is not fully real. The temporal view of reality is a partial, limited, human view of a reality which is not itself limited by time, but includes time within itself. Reality is not simply what exists at a fleeting instant. Nor is it merely the sum of all instants. Nor is it timeless, in the sense that time is not a factor in it at all. Nor is it something everlasting, changeless, static. In some manner it is *more* than temporal. It embraces all the stages of the whole process, yet somehow it embraces them *as process*, though eternally.

It is sometimes objected against the metaphysics of Absolute Idealism that, in denying the reality of time, it takes all the life and movement out of the universe, or that it gives us a " block universe " which is complete and static. In this respect it is contrasted with the metaphysics of Bergson, in which change is real. I cannot feel that this objection is justified. Any philosophy worthy of the name must reckon with both these conflicting aspects of our experience, both the reality of change and the eternal reality within which change is comprised. Bertrand Russell has said " There is some sense, easier to feel than to state, in which time is an unimportant and superficial character of reality." A philosophy which ignores this fact is as unsatisfactory as one which explains away time and change. Hegel does his best to do justice both to the temporal and the eternal. Of course he fails to give a coherent account of them. But who has succeeded ?

Though in Hegel's theory time is not fully real, great stress is laid on the concept of development. Every particular fact is an expression of other facts, and to be understood it must be understood historically. Hegel believed that the process of human history, and, indeed, the process of the whole universe, was systematic through and through, and dominated by a formative principle. History may be regarded, in the temporal and only partially true view, as the process by which " God," or the growing system of universal experience, reaches full self-consciousness. As Hegel had no sense of the astronomical magnitudes of time and space, human history bulked much more largely in his philosophy than seems plausible to us. He regarded mankind as a growing organism whose career was the central theme of the universe. He believed that every stage in humanity's growth was the logical outcome of the previous stage, and that a purpose was unfolding itself from age to age. He had no conception of the prodigious confusion, fortuitousness, precariousness of historical development. He was confident that although reason might sometimes be difficult to discover in the course of events, it must be there. Not only so, but he undertook to deduce the whole universe in all its concreteness from the most abstract of all categories, the concept of mere " being."

This leads us once more to Hegel's famous " dialectical method," which we first noted in connection with his theory of history, and subsequently in connection with Economic Determinism. We must now consider it in relation to the metaphysics of Absolute Idealism. According to Idealism, it will be remembered, every idea is only partially true, and is said to involve its opposite. From the conflict of the two ideas (" thesis " and " antithesis ") emerges a new idea (the " synthesis ") which comprises harmoniously the truth of both the others. This synthesis in turn forms a new thesis which generates a new antithesis; and from the new conflict arises a still more comprehensive synthesis. And so on indefinitely.

This movement of thought Hegel believed to be the basic principle for understanding not only the connections of abstract ideas and the process of history, but also the nature of the universe as a whole. For, though the dialectic is essentially a principle of thinking, it is also, in his view, a principle which applies to the whole of reality; since reality itself is constituted of thought.

One very important application of the dialectical principle, according to Hegel, is the relation of the knower to the object known, or of the self to the not-self. The self has no being without its opposite, the not-self; and in his view the not-self has no being without the self as its knower. The two are opposed to each other, yet they involve each other. From this opposition of abstract self and abstract not-self arises the synthesis of the concrete act of knowledge which embraces both self and not-self. Indeed, the concrete act of knowledge is logically prior to the two abstractions which are derived from it, namely, the self and the not-self. Similarly the timeless Absolute is logically prior to all the particular finite things which we experience in it.

The basic principle of the dialectic may be taken as a denial of a principle of formal logic, namely, that a thing cannot both be and not be. This principle, Hegel says, is true only of static things; not of developing things, which, because they are changing, are always both being and not being.

Applying the dialectical method to the concept of " being," the simplest of all concepts, Hegel points out that a thing cannot *merely* be. Pure being is nothing. A thing must be something definite, determinate. This logically involves its *not being* other things. To be solid involves *not* being liquid. Thus a thing's being what it is is constituted by all that it is not. These contradictory ideas, " being " and " not-being," find their synthesis, as we have seen, in the idea which includes them both, namely " becoming." In ceasing to be what it was, a thing becomes something new. This is the first step of the process by which Hegel believes that he can deduce the whole concrete universe.

We need not consider the stages by which he attempted to pass from pure being to his detailed philosophy of nature. We can see now that it is impossible to deduce the physical world from any such abstraction. The physical world can be known only by observing it.

By the same dialectical method he claimed to deduce the philosophy of mind or spirit. We have already noticed Hegel's dialectical account of the evolution of society, and his political and moral philosophy. Here we are concerned only with criticism of Hegel's fundamental metaphysical principles. What, then, of the dialectic as a metaphysical principle? The main criticism is not that it is untrue, but that as a method of exploration it is barren. Even if reality is in fact such that an all-powerful intellect could deduce it in its full concreteness from some basic concept, neither Hegel nor any other human being can do so; for the good reason that we cannot conceive an adequate basic concept. Hegel's deduction from the concept of " being " is unconvincing from start to finish. Clearly in Hegel's hands the dialectical principle is doomed to failure because it amounts merely to an attempt to deduce the concrete universe from certain abstract characteristics of human language.

(d) *Other Types of Idealism.*—Hegel's philosophy is essentially intellectualistic. The nature of reality is to be discovered through study of the nature of thinking. We must now glance at a kind of idealism in which not thought but will is the key to the understanding of reality. Hegel's younger contemporary and rival, Schopenhauer, reverted to Kant's distinction between the thing in itself and its appearances. He agreed with Kant that the reality behind appearances could not be known by reasoning, but he suggested that it was *probably* very like the reality that we know at first hand in ourselves. And in his view the inner essence that a man knows as " himself " is " will." His body is merely the objective side of his will. Thus the nutritive organs are objectified hunger. The brain is the objectification of the will to know. The root of knowledge itself is will, for we think because we *will* to know, and we will to know because we will to act. (Thus did Schopenhauer enunciate a principle which was to play a great part in subsequent philosophy.) Not only man, but all that exists, is in essence will, or striving. This is the inner nature of the huge turmoil of the physical world. Reality is Will. And the will that is reality is one. Multiplicity is merely an illusion of the human intelligence.

Will arises from want, from deficiency and suffering. When satisfaction comes, desire ceases. But there is no satisfaction for the infinite craving which is Reality. Life, therefore, and all existence is an evil. Pleasure is a mere phantom; for, when desire is satisfied, pleasure vanishes, and before it is satisfied, we are tormented. Salvation comes only when we crush out all desire. In resignation alone we triumph; and the supreme resignation is the extinction of all consciousness, the heaven of annihilation. Thus, in contrast with the calm beatitude, some would say complacency, of the Absolute Idealist, Schopenhauer offers only black pessimism.

Since the time of Schopenhauer Idealism has consisted mainly of a development of the thought of Hegel, who dominated European philosophy throughout most of the nineteenth century. Hegel bequeathed to his followers two ideas that he never properly reconciled, namely, the idea of the perfect, all-inclusive, static

Absolute, in which change is illusory, and the idea of the importance of Development. On the whole, Hegel's English followers, particularly Bosanquet and Bradley, stressed the Absolute. In Italy, however, a new school arose, which abandoned the Absolute and stressed Development. For Croce and Gentile the only reality is not a timeless absolute spirit but an active, changing, self-creative spirit. I have not space to trace the development of these two themes of monistic Idealism.

IV. MATERIALISM

(a) *Mechanical Materialism.*—Having considered the two main types of Idealism, namely pluralistic and monistic, we must turn to Materialism. Two principles are generally regarded as essential to Materialism of every kind. The first is that matter, or what we experience as matter, is more fundamental than mind, or than anything in the nature of our experiencing. The second principle common to all kinds of Materialism is determinism. It is conceived that all events happen systematically and follow necessarily from the nature and mutual relations of the material units. Within the field of Materialism we must distinguish two kinds of theory. One, which may be called Mechanical Materialism, is whole-heartedly materialistic. The other, Dialectical Materialism, is much more temperate and much more subtle.

One of the main sources of Materialism is the work of Herbert Spencer, but his philosophy is not easy to classify. He regarded natural science as the only feasible method of studying reality; and thus he was a champion of Scientific Positivism. He believed that human behaviour and human ideals could in theory be fully described in terms of natural science, and that the complex is always fully describable in terms of the simple. In this sense he was a Mechanical Materialist. But he also tells us that, if we had to choose between translating mental phenomena into physical phenomena and translating physical into mental, the latter would be more acceptable; since our knowledge of matter is derived from " feelings." In this mood, in fact, he abandons materialism for idealism. Further, though a champion of mechanism, he is also a champion of evolution and of a hierarchy of levels of biological development from lifeless matter to man. And the principle by which he judges the level of an organism is the principle of integration. Those organisms are more developed in which the parts are more specialised and more dependent upon one another. In thus emphasising unity-in-difference, or " organicity," he is the pioneer of the biologically inspired philosophies. But in his combination of determinism with degrees of development in integrative behaviour he is a forerunner of Dialectical Materialism.

The crudest kind of Materialism is that according to which the universe consists of a vast collection of ultra-microscopic physical units endowed with force, and interacting in regular manners, such that in theory all events in the universe could be predicted from full knowledge of the nature of the units and their arrangement at any moment. Theoretically all that has to be done is to form inductive laws describing how the different kinds of units behave in relation to one another in very simple situations. From this knowledge all else should be deducible. Not only all physical eve nts but also all mental events, are thought of as in some mysterious way consequences of the nature of the ultimate physical units. Consciousness is at most a strange and ineffectual " glow " produced by the material machinery of the body. One school, the extreme kind of Behaviourists, have even argued that there is no such thing as consciousness; there are only nerves, muscles, glands, and their physical behaviour.

Such is the crudest kind of Materialism, but with the advance of science the concept of matter has been transformed, so that nerves, muscles, glands have come to seem very tenuous. An atom is no longer a little grain endowed with force. It is analysable into a system of electrons, protons, and so on; and these are conceived sometimes as " particles of electricity," sometimes as " wave-trains." The concept of force has been abandoned. Even the concept of energy, the potentiality of doing work, has been discarded (so I understand) in favour of something more abstract and less anthropomorphic. Probing further and further in search of the ultimate physical reality, science has abolished more and more of the concrete, and is apparently left with nothing but waves of the probability that certain occurrences of unknowable quality will happen in definite spatial and temporal relations with other such occurrences. This is indeed a far cry from old-fashioned materialism.

Not only so, but also the old concept of discrete units or particles interacting has tended to give way to the concept of a *field*, *within* which, or in relation to the totality of which, events occur. They are what they are in relation to the rest of the field. And for some purposes the relevant field is the whole universe. Thus in physical science itself Pluralistic Materialism has developed a strong tendency toward monism.

Finally, the scientific Theory of Relativity has led some physicists to believe that the observing mind itself plays a creative part in determining what shall be observed. Such seemingly objective facts as the measurable size of an object and the simultaneity of events are found to vary with the relative motion of the observer. It is therefore argued that all events are events *to* or *for* observing *minds*. The existence of events, we are told, depends on their being observed. Thus has materialistic science delivered itself over to Subjective Idealism.

Many scientists reject the view that the facts of Relativity support subjectivism. They point out that even though size and simultaneity do depend on the relative physical motion of the observer, there is no evidence that they depend on his *observing*, or his mentality. A lifeless camera-plate would record the same kind of results. Many philosophers consider that the arguments on which this new subjectivism is based are confused and mistaken, and, moreover, that they have long ago been refuted. This is not the place to reopen the whole question of Epistemological Realism, which we have already discussed and judged tentatively to be sound.

Modern physicists with a leaning toward Idealism have put forward an argument against the deterministic aspect of Mechanical Materialism, namely, the argument based on physical indeterminacy, which we have already noticed in discussing science. Rightly or wrongly, this argument also has tended to undermine the old faith in " matter."

But even if we reject the arguments for subjectivism, and for determinism, we must recognise that the mere advance of physical science has transformed Mechanical Materialism into something very different from what it was in the nineteenth century. It is no longer an affair of little hard atoms, like marbles. Though the essence of Materialism may be retained, a more appropriate name for it would be " Physicalism," as opposed to Idealism, or " Mentalism."

The real weakness of Mechanical Materialism or Physicalism lies, as we have seen, in the fact that concepts derived wholly from the study of physical nature are not in fact adequate to describe all kinds of events. We cannot in practice give an account of the Russian Revolution or of art or of intellectual activity solely in terms of physical concepts. In affirming that " in theory " we can do so, the Materialist is merely declaring a faith which he cannot prove, or even render intellectually plausible to anyone who has realised the difficulties. In practice each science studies a particular type of events, and employs special concepts derived from its special field of study. In some cases it is possible to analyse the basic concepts of one science into simpler terms derived from another. Thus in theory chemistry can be reduced to physics. In other cases only a partial reduction can be effected, for instance in physiology. In yet other cases the essential features of the special field cannot be reduced at all to any lower-level concepts; though the higher-level events may be found to vary with lower-level events. Emotion cannot be reduced to chemical concepts, but it does to some extent *vary with* chemical events in the body. In other cases, again, even this concomitance cannot be demonstrated, and the higher-level science must, for the present at least, remain completely autonomous. In this state of affairs the belief that in theory everything can be accounted for in terms of physical concepts is little more than a superstition.

Another and seemingly a very cogent argument against Mechanical Materialism we have already noticed in discussing the problem of mind and body. According to the theory, thoughts are either identical with, or wholly caused by, physical changes in the body. This means that the sequence of thoughts in a rational process is determined not by the logical implications of the object about which we are thinking but simply by physical changes in the brain. But if in thinking we really discover the truth about anything, the course of our thinking *must* be determined by the nature of the object thought about, not merely by bodily events. Otherwise all theorising is invalid, and in particular the theorising which produced the theory of Mechanical Materialism. Thus if Mechanical Materialism is true, all the arguments for it are worthless.

We noticed a possible, but not wholly satisfactory, answer to this argument. The nerve-tracks which determine the course of our thought, and our sense of rationality, it may be said, are themselves a " reflection " of the structure of the environment, which is itself on the whole rational. Thus, after all, thought is to be trusted, and the arguments for materialism are not necessarily worthless. But this is guess-work.

(b) *Dialectical Materialism.*—We can now turn to the more subtle kind of Materialism, namely, that which was founded by Karl Marx. But I must begin by once more warning the reader that my knowledge of Marxian theory is not that of a specialist.

Karl Marx was influenced both by the materialistic tradition of science and, as we have seen, by the dialectical form of idealism originated by Hegel. He wisely escapes the charge that we have made against materialism of the mechanical sort, since he avoids the attempt to account for everything by means of concepts derived from physical science. Instead he postulates qualitatively distinct levels of reality, connected together in the dialectical manner. Though he retains the name " Materialism " to mark his opposition to Hegel's Idealism, his theory is not by any means materialistic in the original narrow sense. It is materialistic only in that it derives its explanatory concepts from the nature of the objective world which mind experiences, not from the nature of mind itself, or of experiencing; and it regards the nature of the objective world as more like matter than like mind.

Dialectical Materialism is said to be a principle or formula by means of which we can discover intelligible order in the data of observation. Further, it is said to be scientific. It rejects all concepts that cannot be derived from scientific observation. Such concepts it labels " metaphysical."

Dialectical Materialism itself is in one sense at least a metaphysical doctrine, since it includes propositions about the essential nature of experienced reality in general, and the connection between different orders of observable reality. Using the distinction made by Kant, we may perhaps say that Dialectical Materialism is a case, not indeed of transcendent metaphysics, but of immanent metaphysics. Though it makes no claim to reveal any *hidden* reality behind the world of ordinary experience, and is not in this sense metaphysical, it does claim that, for the understanding of reality as we experience it, the dialectical process is the master key.

The *kind* of understanding which this master key can provide is said by Marxians to be not metaphysical but scientific, because it affords not a means for merely contemplating reality but a means for practically controlling reality. The purpose of human knowledge, we are told, is not mere knowledge but action, not to know the world but to change it. Knowledge is always relative to human needs to act. Disinterested thought is a fiction. Sheer curiosity is, of course, one motive of action, but it is a minor motive, and is not the driving force of any of the sustained and co-operative efforts of human intellect. Moreover, objective truth for contemplation is a fiction. Knowledge is " true " in so far as it leads to successful action.

In this respect the Marxian theory is identical with Pragmatism. As we have already discussed and rejected Pragmatism we need not spend more time on this aspect of Marxism. We may merely repeat that if bourgeois truth is true only for bourgeois action, then proletarian truth is true only for proletarian action. This tendency, not merely to recognise that some degree of bias is inevitable, but to deny any ultimate distinction between true and false, and actually to glory in bias, is extremely dangerous. It encourages some Marxian enthusiasts to dismiss as mere bourgeois propaganda any theory which they regard as unfavourable to Marxism, or which they simply fail to understand. The glorification of bias is bound to lead to an abandonment of intellectual honesty, and finally to the destruction of civilisation by barbarism.

But there is much more in Marxism than this pragmatical strain. The theory does in practice admit an objective distinction between " true " and " false." The dialectical method is regarded as a means for discovering objective truth about the world; though, of course, the *kind* of truth that it discovers is said to be simply truth useful for action.

Dialectical Materialism may be regarded as a theory of the relation of the sciences to each other, or rather of the fields of objective reality studied by the sciences. While each science is entitled to its own special concepts, it also has its special position in the hierarchy of sciences. Sciences of higher rank cannot be simply reduced to, or explained in terms of, sciences of lower rank, as they must be if Mechanical Materialism is true. The relation between the ranks is said to be of a regular and dialectical type. According to the theory, whenever the internal strains in matter reach a certain measurable degree of intensity there appears a qualitatively new kind of behaviour, in which all the internal contradictions of the former kind are solved in a new " synthesis." The new kind of behaviour cannot be described by the scientific laws formulated for the study of the simpler kind of behaviour, but must be studied on its own merits, for the formation of a science of higher rank. Thus the sciences can be arranged in a hierarchy, extending from physics, through biology and psychology to sociology, the science dealing with the most complex kinds of behaviour of which matter is capable, so far as we know.

It is important, but none too easy, to distinguish

between the hierarchical principle adopted in Dialectical Materialism and that adopted in the biologically-inspired theory of Emergence, which Marxians scornfully reject. In the theory of Emergence, as we have seen, the laws of one level cannot, even in theory, be explained in terms of the laws of a lower level. Real novelty emerges at each higher level. Marxians also insist that in their theory, as opposed to that of Mechanical Materialism, real novelty occurs at each level. Yet they sometimes charge the champions of Emergence with introducing a " mystical " principle, owing to an inveterate bias toward the obscurantism which is necessary for the defence of the capitalist class.

All this is really very perplexing. It looks as though Marxians were trying both to have their cake and eat it. They seem to claim that their theory is at once " non-mechanical " (in the sense that it does not accept the laws of physics as the ultimate explanation of everything) and yet also that it is materialistic (in the sense that any principles which it *does* accept must be regarded as inherent in the nature of " matter "). But if matter is after all not purely physical, if the biological and the mental causal concepts are not reducible to the physical, what is the difference between Dialectical Materialism and Emergence? On the other hand, if they *are* reducible, what is the difference between Dialectical Materialism and Mechanical Materialism?

But to continue, the dialectical principle does not apply only to the relation between distinct sciences, but also within the field of any one science. It is said to explain the sudden qualitative changes, or " changes of phase," that occur when a quantitative change reaches a certain critical point. For instance, when ice is heated, there comes a moment when the ordered ranks of its molecules break down, and the crystalline ice becomes liquid water. Professor Levy has pointed out that such catastrophic and qualitative changes are well known in science, as the culmination of more gradual processes. Such changes the Marxian would describe as dialectical.

Marx's lieutenant, Engels, formulated three laws of Dialectical Change, which, in spite of their difficult language, may be taken to express the essentials of the process. (1) " The transition of quantity into quality " expresses the fact, already noted, that any process of increase culminates in a critical point at which a new quality emerges, and new laws are exemplified. (2) " The interpenetration of opposites " expresses the co-existence and conflict of thesis and antithesis in any dialectical situation. As an example, Professor Levy mentions the condition of science in capitalist society. Capitalism itself generated the vast activity of modern science. But whereas capitalism tends toward high prices and therefore scarcity, science tends to function for plenty, and must in time undermine the very system that created it. (3) " The negation of the negation " expresses the final synthesis in which the negation described by the second law is transcended in a new order. Thus, in the case of science, the negation of science and capitalism will not itself be negated until a new social order emerges in which science can fulfil its power of affording social plenty.

The dialectical process is said to be a case of necessity. It is not *logically* necessary, since the synthesis is not deducible from the *manifest* character of the thesis and antithesis. The synthesis contains real novelty.

None the less, the process is said to be necessary in the scientific sense, since it is regular and predictable. There must therefore be a hidden internal necessity. Causation is not to be thought of as merely " invariable sequence," as it was by Hume, but as necessary though not demonstrably necessary. By observation we can form inductive laws to describe and predict in what lower-level conditions the higher-level behaviour will occur. For instance, we can formulate exact inductive laws to predict when water will boil, ice thaw, and (we are told) when social revolution will occur. Also, we can formulate higher-level inductive laws to describe the manner in which the higher-level behaviour itself will occur. In this purely descriptive sense, at least, the behaviour is deterministic. But also, if I understand it, it is deterministic in the sense that this observable regularity is regarded as an expression of an underlying necessity. If this is a correct interpretation, Dialectical Materialism is obviously not merely a scientific but a metaphysical theory.

But though deterministic, the theory does not simply deny human freedom. Marx insists that men make their own history. Of their own intrinsic nature they choose one course rather than another. Throughout history the wills of individuals are determining factors of all human activity. The laws of psychology and sociology are inductive, descriptive. They tell us how human beings do observably behave. They discover no inner necessity in virtue of which human beings *must* so behave. But human nature and the individual will are observed to be regular; and human behaviour is found to be, within limits, predictable. In the mass, men do desire before all other things food, comfort, and security. Their primary motives are economic. The particular acts of particular individuals are not always predictable, because of the subtlety of the psychological influences concerned. But, as we have seen, in dealing with large social happenings individual idiosyncrasies cancel out, and may be neglected.

Marxians often explain that the only true freedom is that which consists in knowing the laws of social change and working to accelerate their operation. This is reminiscent of the contention of some mediæval philosophers that the only true freedom is freedom to will the will of God. For the Marxist, true freedom to-day consists in (*a*) realising that the massed economic desires of the workers, combined with the inevitable breakdown of capitalism, must lead to social revolution; and (*b*) in voluntarily working as a revolutionary. We are not here concerned with the social theory but with the theory of freedom. And so far as freedom is concerned, I fail to see that a man's *will* is any more free in swimming *with* the current than in swimming *against* it.

I will close this subsection by summarising the main criticisms that, in my view, must be made against Dialectical Materialism as a metaphysical theory.

So far as I can understand it, the theory regards " matter " as an underlying *substance* which " has " physical and mental qualities. Marxists would deny this charge, but not, so far as I can see, with justice. We have already seen that the substance-attribute way of thinking is misleading, though not wholly false.

Though the theory insists that matter may have both physical and mental qualities, it apparently regards the physical qualities as in *some* sense more substantial (or

376

essential to matter) than the physical qualities; since it makes much of the late evolution of consciousness. To this it might be replied that perhaps the more essential qualities of matter only *reveal* themselves (to scientific observation) at a late stage of evolution.

In general, the relation between higher and lower levels remains obscure. It is by no means clear in what sense the connection is necessary, and in what sense genuine novelty appears at each higher level. Nor is it clear whether the causal necessity (on which the theory insists) operates solely on the physical plane or also and independently on the mental plane. If I understand the theory, the mental is not reducible to the physical. But if this interpretation is correct, I fail to see why the priority of the physical should be emphasised.

In spite of these criticisms, however, it is obvious that Dialectical Materialism is in our day one of the main growing points of thought. Perhaps in the future, when a decent society has been established and social passions do not confuse all intellectual issues, Dialectical Materialists will outgrow their habit of imputing mere class-bias to those who criticise their beliefs. Perhaps at the same time they will be content to know that their doctrine is an immensely fertile principle, without insisting that it is gospel truth.

V. THE INFLUENCE OF BIOLOGY

(a) *The Pioneer of Evolutionism.*—Absolute Idealism, though it passes beyond formal logic, is in temper intellectualistic. Mechanical Materialism deals chiefly in concepts derived from physics. Dialectical Materialism is inspired partly by physics but mainly by sociology and economics. We must now turn to a type of philosophy in which the source of inspiration is biological and psychological.

Though Darwin was the pioneer of Evolutionism as a biological theory, Herbert Spencer, as we have seen, was the pioneer of philosophical Evolutionism. But whereas many later philosophers have inclined to regard evolution as involving some definitely non-mechanical principle, Spencer accounts for it as a deterministic expression of natural law. His famous definition of evolution runs as follows: " An integration of matter, and a consequent dissipation of motion; during which the matter passes from an indefinite, incoherent homogeneity, to definite, coherent heterogeneity of structure and function, through successive differentiations and integrations." Interpreting this ponderous formula, we may say that, in his view, evolution consists of (a) *specialisation* of parts and differentiation of their characters, and (b) increasing *interdependence* of parts, in fact system, unity in difference. " Life," he tells us, " is the continuous adjustment of internal relations to external relations." But " life in its essence," he says, cannot be conceived in physico-chemical terms.

Spencer thought that evolution, as he defined it, must necessarily occur. He believed that a chaos of simple units must inevitably become a differentiated system. He insisted on " the instability of the homogeneous." This principle is far from being true. Indeed, in modern science its opposite, the principle of increasing " entropy " or " randomness " and *decreasing* system or organicity is accepted as a universal physical principle.

The fact that evolution has occurred, yet cannot be shown to be necessary, combined with the appearance of seeming novelty at higher evolutionary levels, has led some philosophers to abandon the view that in principle a purely scientific account of evolution can be given. We must now turn to the extreme expression of this view.

(b) *The Life Force Theory.*—Bergson's philosophy is based on a criticism of the mechanistic account of biological evolution and of human behaviour. If evolution is a product simply of minute chance variations and natural selection, as Darwin suggested, how could complete organs, such as eyes, which have no value till they are more or less complete, ever evolve? Bergson argues that gradualism cannot have been the main principle of evolution. There must have been sudden large variations that were generally favourable to survival. Such large variations are known to occur and are called " mutations."

Something positive, Bergson thinks, is needed to explain the continued advance of life. Behind evolution there must be some " *élan vital* " or Life Force, making ever new experiments.

In criticism we must note at once certain important points. Eyes, we are now told, have evolved by stages each of which afforded some slight advantage to the organism. One early stage consisted of a sense organ under the skin with a vaguely transparent " blister " of fluid immediately over it. As to mutations, they are more often harmful than beneficial. Indeed, most of them, it seems, are positively lethal. Selection would account for the survival of the beneficial ones.

On the other hand, we must admit that some positive cause is required to explain progressive variation. It is pointed out that the mean around which variations vary in each generation does not advance from one generation to another. If two persons above the average stature have children, the statures of the children vary (in ordinary conditions) not round the parental heights but round the average height for the stock that produced the parents. To explain an evolutionary increase of stature we should have to show how the average stature (round which variations varied) increased from generation to generation. Natural selection prunes the evolutionary tree; but some positive force must provide the sprouting. This is a point in Bergson's favour.

Bergson further argues that evolution cannot be accounted for simply by the gradual adaptation of the organism to the environment. If it could, he says, evolution would have stopped long ago, when all the species were exactly adapted to their environments. To this argument the answer is that perfect adaptation never occurs in an advancing species, because the environment itself is constantly changing. When the environment ceases to change, stagnation does often ensue. Thousands of species have never evolved beyond a primitive level.

Bergson claims that certain psychological facts are incompatible with the theory that living things are mere pieces of mechanism. He cites the " vicarious functioning " of brain tracts; but, as we have already seen, this argument is of doubtful value. He also claims that the facts of abnormal psychology occur without any corresponding brain changes. This certainly cannot be proved. He further claims that subconscious mental activity is inconceivable if consciousness is associated with brain changes. But why? Some brain tracts may sometimes function in dissociation from others.

Bergson's conclusion is that the brain is merely the instrument of consciousness, or the point at which consciousness enters into and avails itself of matter. He suggests that consciousness itself, for its own purpose, evolved the brain. And consciousness itself *is* the Life Force, which is responsible both for the evolution of the race and for the growing of the individual. This would seem to imply that we should be conscious of the process by which we grow up; but we are not.

In Bergson's view consciousness is not the passing activity of an enduring self or " ego." The self *is* the flux of consciousness. We change unceasingly, and even the static is nothing but change of a special kind. The whole universe is change. The universe, he says, is a stream of change, or " becoming," or evolving. There is no Absolute Reality which is the eternal source of change. There is just the continuous flux, without beginning, and without end.

Like Marx, Bergson condemns intellectual metaphysics; but, unlike Marx, he claims that there is another kind of metaphysics, not of intellect but of " intuition." By means of " intuition," which is said to be instinct conscious of itself, we realise in our own changing consciousness the reality which is also the reality of the universe. For we *are* the " becoming " or " duration " or " *durée* " which reality is.

Bergson distinguishes experienced duration from the intellectual abstraction which we call " time," and use for scientific purposes. This abstract " time," or " mathematical time," is a system of temporal relations between events. If real time, or " duration," were to be speeded up, the system of relations would not reveal the fact, since they would remain the same. Clocks, like everything else, would go quicker. In distinction from mere " scientific time," duration itself is the continuous progress of the past which " gnaws into the future," and is lived through in our consciousness.

Just as intellect dissects the living duration into the abstract instants and dates of scientific time, so also it dissects our concrete spatial experience into distinct material objects. Matter is said to be the falsifying view of reality, created by intellect. The shapes of things do not belong to reality itself. They are the pattern which intellect projects upon reality as an aid to action. Intellect " carves out " these solid and distinct objects, constructs them, as one constructs a formula for action.

In the same way, Bergson says, intellect gives a falsifying account of motion. It analyses motion into a series of static states, like the instantaneous views that make up a cinematograph film. It misses entirely the reality of motion, which only intuition can grasp as it really is.

He admits, however, that matter is not *wholly* the creature of intellect. For there is *something* which is other than the intuited flow of life, and something with which intellect is specially concerned. What precisely this " other " is he never clearly tells us. Sometimes he speaks of it as a flow in the opposite direction from life. It is the falling and extinguished remains of life's rocket. Or if life is the rising jet of a fountain, matter is the falling drops, some of which collide with the upthrust of the jet.

The peculiar nature of intellect, Bergson argues, throws light on the free-will controversy. The special function of intellect is to abstract. Any single act of volition is an abstraction formed by intellect. What is real is not isolated acts but the indivisible flow of life. Each act, regarded in isolation, inevitably appears as determined by causes beyond itself. But the personality as a whole is freely creative in every moment. Free will is creative action. This view, says Bergson, is supported by the fact that in practice we never really believe in determinism. We confidently *feel* ourselves free.

Bergson's work has played a great and salutary part in the formation of modern thought. It was a symptom of the revolt against mechanism, and against intellectualism of the doctrinaire kind. It helped men to realise that the scope of intellect, even of the ideally perfected intellect, had grave limitations, and that intellectual analysis might miss the essence of the object analysed.

But, as we have seen, some of Bergson's arguments are far from convincing; and his theories are unsatisfactory. In particular they are open to the charge that they defeat themselves. They claim to prove that intellect is in principle a false guide, save in practical matters; but since they themselves are based on intellectual processes, their own conclusions must be invalid. The sweeping condemnation of intellect and praise of intuition, though a healthy reaction from crude intellectualism, is itself crude. As we have seen, intellect and intuition involve one another. Intellect itself moves by intuitive leaps, and intuition is often the outcome of preparatory intellectual work.

We have already considered and dismissed the theory

that intuition is " instinct conscious of itself," and that it affords a more penetrating knowledge than intellect. When instinct is " conscious of itself " it is not so much a conscious knowing as a conscious doing. Its knowing is a very limited awareness of the particular stimuli which evoke it, and a generally quite imprecise awareness of the actual response. In what other sense does the angry man know the situation that makes him angry, or know the activity of anger itself ? What reason is there to suppose that the instinctive bird or insect knows in any more effective way ? It simply behaves " by blind instinct."

Another difficulty in Bergson's philosophy is the theory that reality is featureless. If all the forms that we know in the material world are purely subjective, how is it that we are compelled to perceive things as having certain characters and not others ? Why is the reality of a cat cat-like and not tree-like ? Must we not admit that however illusory our perception, *some* differences must actually belong to reality itself as the causes of the differences in our perception ?

(c) *Vitalism and Emergence.*—Many philosophers who are unable to accept the extravagant anti-intellectualism of Bergson have nevertheless been greatly influenced by the biological temper which he so persuasively advocated. Here it is impossible to do more than note the general trend of this great stream of philosophical thought, ignoring its many meanderings and the wealth of ideas that have flourished along its banks.

The controlling principles of philosophies of this type would seem to be three, and all are derived from biology. They are: the concept of *evolution*, the concept of *teleology*, and the concept of *organism*.

Evolution is conceived as a cosmical process, tending, either by necessity or more often as an undecided free adventure, toward something like a " far-off divine event " in which the potentiality in the universe for consciousness will be fulfilled by a process continuous with biological evolution. For instance, in the philosophy of Samuel Alexander, the universe is said to have a " *nisus* toward deity," a tendency or urge or bias to achieve the fully awakened cosmical consciousness. In this view space and time, or rather space-time, is regarded as the fundamental reality, which generates the manifold characters of the universe. This is a very different conception from that of Absolute Idealism, in which reality is " above " space and time.

Teleology, in the philosophies of organism, is contrasted with mechanism. According to the Vitalists, since evolution cannot be explained in terms of mere natural selection, it is necessary to postulate a purposive Life Force, a metaphysical substance, controlling the whole movement of evolution; or a number of particular " entelechies " or purposive substances controlling the growth of individual organisms. By some such means, they argue, it is ensured that on the whole biological variations shall have a bias favourable to progressive evolution.

This theory, which C. D. Broad has called " Substantial Vitalism," must be contrasted with what he has called " Emergent Vitalism." According to Lloyd Morgan, it is a mistake to conceive such distinct teleological substances, but we must recognise that, when physical units are organised in a certain degree of complexity, they manifest a new mode of behaviour, which is different from mechanical behaviour, and must be called " teleological," in that it is determined partly by a goal, or end to be attained. The new kind of behaviour is said to " emerge " in the complex situation. In judging the theory Broad gives a very useful analysis of the idea of teleology. The structure or behaviour of anything is said to be " teleological " if it cannot, even in theory, be fully described without introducing an end. The thing must be fashioned *as if*, or must behave *as if*, it had been purposefully designed to attain that end. The structure or plan of a man-made machine is obviously teleological in this sense, though its *behaviour* can be described fully in terms of mechanism. This is a case of " external teleology," which is contrasted with the " internal teleology " of a living organism. Organisms seem like machines that make themselves. In the case of a living organism the champion of mechanism may reasonably claim that *behaviour* is in theory reducible to mechanism (i.e. the physical functioning of mechanical parts); but it is difficult for him to explain by means of pure mechanism the form of *structure*, or plan, of the organism, in virtue of which its parts may be thought of as functioning mechanically so as to attain the ends of survival and reproduction. According to the Emergence theory, then, teleology " emerges " out of mechanism. Similarly, at a higher level of organisation conscious purposiveness is said to emerge out of unconscious teleology. So to speak, it is " teleological behaviour become conscious of itself," and therefore capable of more flexible and accurate adaptation to the environment.

In terms of this concept of teleology these philosophers describe the evolution of species and the instinctive behaviour of individual organisms. And sometimes they suppose that teleology, thus defined, is in some sense a potentiality of the universe as a whole in its evolution toward a state of perfected organicity and consciousness.

A final decision about Emergent Vitalism cannot be reasonably made until much more biological evidence has been accumulated. It is still possible that a complete account not only of behaviour but of the evolution of species may be given in terms of mechanism. But we must recognise that no such account of evolution has yet been given.

It remains true, however, that so far as size, shape, and movement are concerned the concept of mechanism is *in theory* capable of explaining evolution and behaviour. On the other hand, as we have already seen, a concept which itself contains nothing but size, shape, and movement cannot, logically, account for anything else. It cannot account for secondary qualities. Nor can it account for consciousness. The most it can do is to describe the mechanical situations in which these are observed to occur, or emerge.

It is worth noting, by the way, that the theory of Emergent Vitalism does not necessarily deny determinism, though its advocates often do in fact deny it. There is no reason why the emergent teleological factor should not turn out to be (if we had more precise knowledge of it) perfectly regular and predictable. Its actual emergence, though not logically derivable from the lower-level, mechanical laws, might occur precisely in certain mechanical situations and not in others; and therefore it would be determinate. And when once it had emerged, its operation might be perfectly systematic.

It must not be supposed that the emergent factor, so to speak, " descends from the blue " like a divine messenger. Rather we must suppose that it is always a latent capacity in the mechanical units, but a capacity which cannot manifest itself save when they occur in certain complex relations with one another.

(d) *Whitehead's Philosophy.*—The third of the controlling principles which appears in philosophies of a biological temper is the concept of " organism," which first came into prominence in the work of the Absolute Idealists, and was developed in a very different manner by Herbert Spencer.

An organism is a system in which the character of each part is determined by its relation to the rest of the system. A system can be either more or less organic in comparison with other systems. The character of a part can be either more thoroughly or less thoroughly determined by its relations to the rest of the system. The ideal limit in one direction is the " system " in which the parts are wholly unaffected by one another, like Leibniz's monads. In the other direction is the ideal limit in which the parts are wholly determined by their relations, as in the Hegelian Absolute. Both these extremes are impossible abstractions. If they are to be avoided it is necessary to allow that the parts may be in some respects unaffected by their relationship, and in others affected intrinsically by it. A biological organism is plainly organic in this sense. In philosophies that make great use of the concept of organism it is sometimes contended that the whole universe either is or is tending to become organic.

The philosophy of A. N. Whitehead is perhaps the most thorough-going and the most striking philosophy of organism. Unfortunately, Whitehead's work, though rich in suggestive ideas which open up vistas of novel and significant thought, is often very obscure. I do not pretend to be able to judge how far the obscurity is due to actual confusion of thought and how far to the inability of the ordinary mind to share the insight which has gone to the making of this remarkable philosophy. My own experience in reading Whitehead has been rather like that of an explorer groping his way through dense jungle. Now and then he emerges upon some bare mountain-top, to be rewarded by a panorama that embraces seemingly a whole virgin continent, the home, perhaps, of a future civilisation.

Not that Whitehead's work is novel in any revolutionary manner. He himself deprecates the modern tendency to break away from the great stream of philosophical speculation. He insists that philosophy must speculate, and must take note of past speculations. His own work, he suggests, is but " a transformation of some main doctrines of Absolute Idealism on to a a realistic basis." (Might not this be said also of Dialectical Materialism ?)

Whitehead's starting-point is a criticism of the analytic method of modern science. As a method of practical scientific enquiry it is, of course, invaluable; but it led, almost unconsciously, to a false metaphysics in which certain factors in the concrete world were abstracted from their setting and regarded as the " reality," of which all the rest was subjective "appearance." This error Whitehead calls the fallacy of " illicit abstraction." It led to Descartes' dualism, which Whitehead describes as the " bifurcation " of nature into material and mental characters, and the attempt to explain everything in terms of the material. Those who felt that this kind of explanation was all wrong were themselves guilty of " bifurcation," since on their side they attempted to explain everything either in terms of the other illicit abstraction, namely the mental, or in terms of the interaction of the two distinct abstractions, matter and mind.

Bifurcation also led, according to Whitehead, to a false separation of substance and quality, culminating in theories of an unknowable reality and its appearances. In yet another respect it led to error, namely, in the sharp distinction between the " thing " and its " environment," a failure to recognise that the two are not substantially distinct, but intimately intermingled. According to Whitehead, it is always a mistake to abstract a thing from its environment and to think of this abstraction as concrete. He calls this error the fallacy of " misplaced concreteness." Rejecting this analytic kind of philosophy, Whitehead offers a system based on the conviction that everything is intrinsically related to everything else, or is constituted by its relations to everything else. The result is a far-reaching monism, but a monism that differs from Absolute Idealism in at least three important respects. In the first place, reality is not a static, timeless reality. It is actually going on. It is essentially process, though it has, as we shall see, an eternal aspect. Secondly, reality is not featureless, as it was for some Idealists. It really has (though often not simply in the manner that we suppose) the features that we perceive it as having. Thirdly, according to Whitehead, reality is to be conceived not in terms of thought but of " feeling." (Some Idealists would agree with this.) Feeling, however, is not, in Whitehead's view, purely mental or subjective. It has also an objective aspect which is essentially what we mean by " material."

Every particular " thing " or " event " in the universe, whether an electron or a man or an explosion or an epoch of civilisation or the career of a star, is in some sense constituted by its relations to the rest of the universe. These relations are not merely of the logical type, as in Hegel's system. They are relations of *feeling*. Everything feels, or perceives, or takes account of, everything else.

Only in highly organised things, such as men, is this feeling a conscious feeling. Elsewhere it is subconscious. In passing we must note that " subconscious feeling " is a very slippery phrase. The word " consciousness " itself is ambiguous. It may mean any sort of awareness, or it may mean something more, perhaps " awareness *plus* awareness-of-that-awareness." Then " subconscious feeling " is simply awareness, *without* awareness-of-the-awareness.

Every particular thing, then, is sensitive to other things in the sense that it grasps aspects of other things, and is itself constituted by what it grasps of other things. This relationship Whitehead calls " prehension." Every event is a " prehensive occasion " embodying the relations of that event to the rest of the universe.

This sensitivity toward the rest of the universe is not, however, a thing's whole being. It is not only a passive receiving but also an active giving. Its whole being is constituted by its reception of the rest of the universe in its particular place and time, *and* its contribution to the rest of the universe throughout all space and time.

As we have already seen, Whitehead denies that a thing is " simply located " in a particular place and time. It *is* the sum-total of what we call its " effects " throughout space and time, *plus* its reception of the " effects " of the rest of the universe in its simply-located focal point (or rather its focal region) in space and time.

The words " thing " and " event " are, of course, misleading. We must think of the universe as a seamless (but not featureless) unity, which for our own interest we can analyse into discrete things. Similarly a cube may theoretically be analysed into an infinite number of lesser cubes, some of them concentric with others, some overlapping, some distinct from one another. A better image, perhaps, is the multitude of spreading circles made by raindrops on a pond. But, to complete the image, the circles must be infinite in number, and every abstract point must both radiate and receive influences.

And what of the characters in respect of which things differ and are alike ? Whitehead distinguishes between particulars and universals, but he does not hypostatise either of these abstractions; and he does not use the words " particular " and " universal." An " event " is any particular happening (long or short) in the spatio-temporal world. But apart from the abstract spatio-temporal characters which constitute an event, it has also the qualities which we either perceive or intellectually know it to have. These universal qualities he calls, rather oddly, " eternal objects." The word " object " indicates that they are objective, that they are not mere subjective " ideas " in our minds, or God's mind. The word " eternal " indicates that, like the Platonic "forms," they are in a sense not restricted by time and space, since they may occur anywhere and anywhen. But unlike the Platonic forms, they are not fully real independently of their particular occasions. They have only the kind of reality which a *possibility* has. Together, in their infinite variety, they constitute the infinite realm of possibility. Though they are mere abstractions, they are said to have "ingression" into, or be "ingredient" in, the flux of events. That is, certain "eternal objects" characterise certain events.

An event is characterised by certain "eternal objects" and not others. If it were characterised by all, it would have no character at all. "Every actual occasion is a limitation imposed on possibility." The actual world, then, must be given definite form in virtue of some principle of limitation. This principle of limitation Whitehead calls God. But God, regarded in this aspect, is a very strange God, who is not a concrete being, but an abstraction. Regarded thus, he has no reality save as a principle characterising the universe. In this aspect, he is not actual, but is "the ground for concrete actuality." He is "the principle of concretion." His existence is said to be "the ultimate irrationality." No reason can be given for his nature, or for the actualisation of just those possibilities that are actualised and not others. But, as we shall presently see, God has also another aspect.

We have seen that every actual thing or event is said to be a "prehensive occasion," constituted by its relations to other events. To this conception we must now add the doctrine of "negative prehension." A thing's positive character is what it is partly in virtue of all the characters that it is *not*. A cat is a cat partly in virtue of *not* being winged, finned, handed, and so on. The cat, therefore, negatively prehends all the characters which are excluded from it. Similarly all " living " things, in being alive and not lifeless, negatively prehend the " non-living " character of lifeless matter.

The difference between " alive " and " lifeless " is for Whitehead only a difference of degree, not an absolute difference. All actual things are organisms. Biology is the study of the larger organisms, physics the study of the smaller. The whole universe is a living process, not in the sense that it is a single living organism, but as entirely composed of an infinity of interpenetrating living organisms of all degrees of complexity. And an organism, as we have seen, is essentially an " occasion of experience."

But the experience which constitutes a thing is not simply passive. It is active; and active in two ways, if I understand Whitehead rightly. Not only is a thing active in that it contributes to the nature of all other things, but also in that it has its own " subjective aim," its striving to fulfil its potentiality. In virtue of this " subjective aim " it incorporates certain possible prehensions into itself and rejects others. More precisely, it accepts everything; but in virtue of its " subjective aim," some relations play a more important part in its make-up than others.

God also is said to have a " subjective aim." For God is not *simply* an abstraction. He is not *merely* the primordial " principle of concretion " in virtue of which the universe actually occurs. He has not only a " primordial " but also a " consequent " nature. He is not only the beginning but the end; or, better, not only the ground or root but the flower of all existence. For " he shares with every new creation its actual world." Thus he has, after all, actuality. " Each temporal occasion embodies God "; and God is " a multiplicity of actual components in process of creation." Not only so, but God is one. For the fulfilment of God's " consequent nature " is a single consciousness, and " the realisation of the actual world in the unity of his nature." Between God and the world there is a reciprocal relation. Each is necessary to the other's being. By reason of this reciprocal relation, " the love in the world passes into the love in heaven, and floods back into the world. In this sense, God is the great companion—the fellow-sufferer who understands."

It is all too likely that the foregoing brief account of Whitehead's philosophy is far more inadequate and misleading even than I know it to be. But I could not complete this book without some account of the most brilliant, most comprehensive, most significant, though also most difficult, metaphysical system of our time.

It is impossible here to offer anything but the briefest criticism. The whole system is founded on the doctrine of intrinsic relations, the doctrine that particular things are constituted by their relations with other things. As we have seen, the objection to this doctrine is that relations presuppose terms. If we analyse the terms away into more relations nothing whatever is left. To this objection Whitehead would reply that he has insisted on the actuality of the particular " occasions " in space and time which support the relations. In this view both relations and terms are abstractions, and neither must be hypostatised and used as an all-sufficient explanatory concept.

Apart from the general criticism that it is sometimes impossible to tell whether Whitehead is being very profound or very vague, we must note also that sometimes, for instance in his theory of God, the trend of his argument seems to be determined less by logical necessity than by the desire to complete his system by relating it, in however strange a manner, with religious orthodoxy.

However this may be, the sympathetic reader will discover in his works a degree of metaphysical imagination and insight which far more than compensates for any shortcomings.

CHAPTER XII

CONCLUSIONS

I. Conclusions thus far.   II. Time.   III. Mysticism.

I.   CONCLUSIONS THUS FAR

I SHALL begin this chapter with a summary of the positive though tentative conclusions which seem to me to have emerged at one stage or another throughout the course of this book.   I shall then give a brief account of two metaphysical problems which I regard as the growing points of metaphysical enquiry to-day.   I mean the problems of Time and Mystical Experience.

Our discussion of personal immortality led to the conviction that no such possibility should be allowed to play a guiding part in the conduct of a man's life. Enquiring into the relation of mind and body, we came to no clear conclusion, save the surmise that they must not be regarded as distinct substances.   The problem of the external world and the experient led us into deep waters, but left us with a sense of the rich actuality of a universe that was no mere creature of our minds.

Our examination of the nature of reasoning suggested the conclusion that the method of intellectual enquiry was in principle capable of yielding objectively true propositions about unexperienced regions of the world.   With some hesitation we rejected the uncompromising view that logical implication was a purely linguistic phenomenon, that it applied only to the analysis of definitions or concepts, and in no sense to the external world.   We decided that, in so far as a concept was superficially true of the world, the deeper logical implications of it might reasonably be expected to be true also. But we admitted that there was no *necessity* in this, even if the initial concept itself was true of the world. The implications could not be more than *probably* true of the world. As a matter of fact they were often borne out in practice.

In the field of ethics we found that no classical theory was satisfactory, but on the other hand we came to the opinion that radical ethical scepticism was unjustified. In spite of Logical Positivism, we regarded moral experience as affording a sense of objectivity and universality which should not be overlooked in the interest of any theory. We really do experience free activity as *good* and frustration as *bad* in the fundamental and indefinable sense.

Examination of the nature of personality led us to think of the individual as a system of capacities of varying degrees of complexity and mental lucidity; and of individuals as differing from one another in sensitivity, discrimination, and integration. We distinguished between the distinctively animal and the distinctively human capacities, and those obscure capacities which seem to lie at the upper reaches of human nature.

In particular, we distinguished between the distinctively animal and the distinctively human modes of social behaviour. Further analysis led us to contrast the herd-mentality (the animal mode) with the individualistic mentality and the will for genuine community. In human society, we decided, individualism mostly dominates, but herd-mentality is always present and sometimes dominant; while the will for genuine community is precarious and rare, though sometimes crucially important. We examined theories of social change, and decided that Economic Determinism was by far the most significant. We saw reason, however, to refrain from setting it up as an absolutely and universally true principle, save in the loosest possible sense.

Passing on to metaphysics, we recognised that the kind of truth which intellect could discover in this sphere was very limited. We had to face the claim that all metaphysical enquiry was necessarily futile because propositions that could not even in theory be verified must be strictly meaningless. In order to judge this claim, we distinguished between " immanent " metaphysics (the attempt to discover by observation and rational analysis the most general characters that are true of anything whatever in the experienced universe, or of the experienced universe as a whole), and " transcendent " metaphysics (the attempt to discover a hidden reality behind experience, and different in kind from it). We decided that immanent metaphysics, though its conclusions must always be suspect, was not in principle impossible. Further, since metaphysical assertions of both types are very common, it seemed desirable to study metaphysics if only in order to be able to expose false metaphysical assumptions and refute false metaphysical theories.

We then attempted a survey of metaphysical theories from Descartes to Whitehead. Descartes' dualism of matter and mind led to Spinoza's monism in which mind and matter are regarded as attributes of a single substance. This in turn led to Leibniz's pluralistic idealism, according to which there is an infinite number of substances, all of them mental, and matter is illusory. Then followed the monistic idealism of Kant and Hegel, in which reality is essentially mental, but is a single, indivisible, quality-less Absolute Spirit. In revulsion from this, came pluralistic and mechanical materialism, in which only the characters studied by physics are real, and reality consists of an infinite number of physical units interacting with one another. On the other hand, Marx's dialectical materialism rejected mechanism. In his view physical categories are not the sole causal characters. Nevertheless, in his view mind has a determinate nature, and all its behaviour is in the long run determined by the dialectical necessities forced upon it by the objective environment, and particularly the social environment. We also examined Bergson's Life Force theory, in which a purposive power controls evolution and human history; in which intellect is essentially falsifying, and the only true knowing is intuitive. For these theories we found little evidence; but we recognised that Bergson was very important as a check upon the extravagant faith in mechanism and rationalism. We then turned to the Emergence theory, in which teleology and consciousness are said to " emerge " in very complex configurations of physical entities. Lack of evidence made it impossible to judge this theory. Finally we examined Whitehead's philosophy, which seeks to harmonise ideas derived from Absolute Idealism, epistemological realism, and biology. This system we found obscure, but full of suggestive ideas.

None of these theories has proved entirely satisfactory, but all have contributed, if only in a negative manner, to our understanding of the experienced world.

A few positive but rather vague conclusions may be offered.

Perhaps we should begin by reminding ourselves that, though abstract thought is capable of yielding important truths about the universe, we have again and again discovered that it involves a characteristic snare. It is all too apt to lead to the hypostatisation of some one kind of factor in the universe and the dismissal of all others as "illusory," or mere "epiphenomena." This procedure has repeatedly led to bad metaphysics. For instance, with regard to the problem of "the one and the many," neither extreme monism nor extreme pluralism can afford us a coherent description of the universe. In fact the universe is both many and one. It is fatal to abstract either its unity or its multiplicity, and hypostatise one of these characters at the expense of the other. Parts cannot be wholly independent of one another, but neither can they be wholly an expression of their relations to one another. However minutely we analyse anything, we shall never be able to show that it consists of certain atomic elements and certain atomic relations. Always the parts will be in principle further analysable into minute wholes consisting of minuter parts which in turn are constituted by their intrinsic relations to other parts. All wholes are infinitely analysable into actual parts ; yet all parts are synthetic systems of intrinsic relations.

Another reasonable conclusion is that neither the mental aspect of experience nor the physical aspect should be abstracted and regarded as an all-sufficient concept for understanding the universe. Metaphysically, mentality is as significant as physicality; and vice versa.

Tentatively we may draw another conclusion, of a different type, which involves not only philosophy but science. There seems some reason to believe that purposiveness, which in one manner or another characterises all conscious behaviour, must play a very large part in the universe. When we remember the size of the physical universe and the immensities of the past and the future, we cannot but believe that, scattered among the myriads of stars, there are, or will be, purposeful beings as superior to us as we are to the amœba. Of these beings we can conceive almost nothing, but from the examination of our own experience we are entitled to draw certain tentative conclusions about them. So far as we know, all conscious beings are essentially active. And when they develop beyond the level of blind impulse, they tend to *desire* the fulfilment of their particular capacities for action. These capacities, as we have seen, vary in complexity and subtlety. And conscious beings also vary in the degree of the integration of their capacities. That is, some conscious beings are more unified, more highly organised than others. It is reasonable to suppose that, throughout the universe, conscious beings vary immensely both in the richness of their capacities and in the degree of integration of their capacities to form unified systems.

Examination of our own human experience has led us to assert that we do recognise differences of intrinsic worth in human beings. In the last analysis these differences of worth correspond to differences of mental development, differences of richness and integration of knowing-feeling-striving. In fact, we tend to admire most those who are most developed as knowers-feelers-strivers, in fact as persons. It was pointed out that both a subjective and an objective account of this value can be given. We may, I suggest, affirm with some confidence that this admiration for personal development is no mere human whim, but a characteristic implicit in the nature of consciousness, and explicit whenever conscious beings reach a certain degree of development, throughout the universe.

Further, as we have seen, conscious beings that have passed beyond a certain stage of mental development tend to desire fulfilment not only for themselves as individuals, but for some other conscious beings who are personally known to them. Moreover, in intercourse with other and diverse persons, they may find immense enrichment of their own personality. Hence emerges the ideal of personality-in-community. As conscious beings advance in mental growth, they come to recognise that this ideal must embrace not merely their own kin or neighbours, not only their tribe or nation, not only the whole race or species, but all conscious beings whatever, no matter how foreign. It is surely probable that this desire for the fulfilment of personality-in-community plays a very large part in the universe. We must remember, of course, that the particular forms which it may take in different kinds of worlds, up and down the universe, may be utterly alien to our comprehension and appreciation. Or rather, not *utterly* alien ; since, if these arguments are correct, there is an essential underlying kinship and identity in all possible kinds of conscious being.

On the whole it seems more reasonable than unreasonable to believe that the ideal of progress in the direction of ever-increasing personality-in-community is not peculiar to man but is a very general characteristic of conscious beings, and is in some manner deeply rooted in the nature of the universe. It is no fixed goal, but one which at the best of times tends to recede faster than it is approached. For the activity of conscious beings produces novel situations in which new forms of personality and of community emerge, and new, hitherto inconceivable capacities demand expression. By means of intelligence and creative imagination conscious beings can sometimes so manipulate reality in the external world and in themselves that it will manifest entirely new aspects of itself. In my earlier book, *Star Maker*, I have sketched an imaginary history of the cosmos on these lines.

In our survey of metaphysics in recent centuries we saw that in one form or another this ideal of personality-in-community was affirmed or implicitly accepted by all the great philosophers. Not only was it accepted as a human aim, but in many cases it was given some kind of metaphysical status. This consensus of opinion may well strengthen our conviction.

Such, I suggest, should be our tentative conclusions, thus far. One famous metaphysical problem we have several times encountered, but we have come to no kind of decision about it. The problem of Time must now be briefly considered on its own merits. In our metaphysical survey we came across two very different attitudes to time, represented, for instance, on the one hand by Hegel, for whom the universe is eternally perfect, and time is but a limited aspect of it, and by Bergson, for whom the passage of our experience is absolutely real, and the static is an abstraction. The problem of time is so important that I must devote a special section to it.

II. TIME

Let us begin by noting briefly how we do in fact experience time. We actually *perceive* changes and movements. The rise of a rocket is not merely *remembered* in successive moments. We actually *see* it soaring. On the other hand, when the process is completed, when the rocket has burst into a shower of stars and has disappeared, we *remember* the vanished past event. In a very fragmentary manner we retain much of our past experience as a system of latent memories. And in addition to our personal memories we have more or less reliable knowledge of other past events. This knowledge is derived from the reports of other persons, from historical, anthropological, geological records, and astronomical observations. Our experience of the future consists, mainly at any rate, of inferences from the present and past. Immediate pre-vision or " second sight " must certainly not be dismissed as too fantastic to be credible. We know of no necessity which renders pre-vision impossible, and there is some fragmentary evidence for it both in waking experience and in dreams. But it would be rash to affirm confidently that it does occur.

Such in brief are the possible forms of our experience of time. It is important to realise that we actually *perceive* change and motion. If our experience were simply made up of a succession of instantaneous flashes, like the separate pictures of a cinematograph film, each coming into being and vanishing, to give place to the next, we should not perceive motion at all, but only *remember* that things *were* different from what they *are*. For the pictures to be fused into living motion, there must be something persisting from instant to instant to do the fusing.

But, of course, the idea of time as made up of timeless instants, or of space as made up of sizeless points, is false. Instants and points are abstractions from our concrete experience of time and space. Indeed, time and space themselves are abstractions from our concrete experience of the " passage " of spatio-temporal events.

To hypostatise the instant and the point is to let ourselves in for a swarm of false problems, such as the ancient puzzle of the flying arrow. The arrow at a certain instant is said to be actually at a certain point. Its tip is " in " a point. If so, at the instant there is no difference between a moving arrow and a stationary arrow. There is no *movement* in a point-instant. If so, how does the arrow ever reach the next point ? The whole difficulty arises from the mistake of abstracting and hypostatising instants and points. If time were literally composed of timeless instants, laid beside one another, so to speak, it would never get under way at all. All the instants would coincide. And if space were a host of sizeless points, either they would all coincide as *one* point, or there would after all have to be spaces between them.

During a very short span of time, then, we actually *perceive* change and motion. This span, which has no clear beginning or end, is called the " specious present," or " now." If a change or motion is too rapid, we do not perceive it at all. The light and dark phases of an electric filament lit by an alternating current are not perceived. On the other hand, equally if a change is too slow, we do not perceive it. For instance, we cannot perceive the movement of the minute hand of a watch. We only remember that it *was* where it *is* not. We may conceive a being who could distinguish the strokes of a bee's wing as we distinguish those of a gull's; or again, a being who could perceive the growing of a tree over a century as we might perceive a quick-motion film of its growth. We may conceive a being whose " now " was a single electro-magnetic pulsation; or one who embraced within his " now " a geological epoch, or an astronomical æon. We may even conceive a being who could *both* distinguish the single vibration and yet also grasp the whole æon as " now "; as we distinguish the individual tones of a melody and yet grasp in one act of perception the whole bar. What we can *not* conceive is a being whose " now " is a time-less instant; or, on the other hand, one whose " now " is eternity. For neither instant nor eternity can accommodate actual " passage."

With regard to memory, we have already had occasion to refer to Bertrand Russell's suggestion that all memory might be sheer illusion. This possibility is based on illicit abstraction. If all that is immediately given in experience is an instant, then not only does movement vanish, but the whole past may be regarded as illusion. But perception of movement and change guarantees *some* sort of past, however different in detail from that retained in our obviously fallible memory.

In considering the philosophy of time we encounter the question whether time constitutes a medium, a matrix, *within* which events happen, somewhat as toy bricks may be packed in a box in successive layers, or whether time is nothing but a particular kind of relation-ship between events. I shall not discuss this question in detail. The idea that time is logically prior to events, and that there might be time without events in it, seems to be another product of illicit abstraction. One might as well suppose that parenthood was logically prior to the individuals that become parents, that it was a medium within which individuals assume parental relations.

Time, then, is best regarded as a relationship of events. The same arguments apply to space. What is concrete is events, which consist of characters in spatial and temporal relations with each other. If so, then the modern conception of space as at once boundless and finite becomes intelligible. We are told that a journey in a straight line among the stars would finally bring one round to one's starting-point. This means merely that the possible spatial relations between events form a closed, not an open and infinite series. Similarly if time consists simply of relations of " before " and " after " and " contemporaneous with," there is no reason why the " last " event of the time series should not also immediately precede the " first." Then the whole series would be " circular." This would not mean an endlessly *repeated* cycle of events, but a single cycle. For there would be no *other*, " straight-line " time-series of events *in* which the cycle could be repeated. I mention these possibilities merely to show that our temporal experience is not as simple as we sometimes suppose.

It is impossible to think accurately about time unless we distinguish two very different aspects of it. From the subjective point of view we regard it as consisting essentially of the *present* event (or " now "), a vaguely remembered or reported *past*, and an expected *future*.

These three modes of subjective time have very different quality or status. The present is always handing over its character to the immediate past and assuming a new character.

From the other, the objective point of view, time consists of the series of events which (in the broadest sense) constitute the actual history of the universe. These are arranged in a certain order. Each is related by the relation " after " to the preceding event, and by the relation " before " to the succeeding event. More accurately, history consists of one long continuous event which can be analysed into an indefinite number of abstract constituent events. From this point of view, which we may regard as the " scientific " aspect of time, all the events have similar status. Past, present, and future are irrelevant.

It is tempting to regard the series of events as in itself timeless or eternal, and our experience as a *passing along* the series, as the beam of a searchlight sweeps over the clouds, illuminating first one and then another feature; or as a stick floating on a river passes stationary objects on the bank. This theory, it is sometimes said, turns time into a purely subjective fact, and therefore an illusion, not a characteristic of reality. But this is a mistake. Even if external events are timeless, the sequence of our illusory mental views of them is a real sequence. The problem of time is merely shifted from the external to the internal sphere of reality. From the scientific point of view, no doubt, the careers of conscious beings are more or less prolonged events in particular situations within the whole tissue of events. The career of a prehistoric man and the career of a future man are just as " real " as one's own present experience. In a certain mood it is impossible not to believe that this is true. But if it *is* true, change, motion, the *passage* of time, become illusions.

On the other hand, if we insist on retaining the absolute reality of passage, the past and future must be non-existent. This raises a difficulty. Reality is reduced to a knife-edge of instant-present events, between two vast non-entities, the past and the future. Or is the present *not* an instant but a small span of time? Then how big a span? To fix on the span of our own specious present is arbitrary.

A special difficulty about the nature of time has been created by modern physics. It has come to seem that time and space are not as distinct as they were thought to be. At any rate their distinction is not as clear as it was. This is not an occasion to discuss the physical theory of relativity, even if I were competent to do so. But a few words must be said about its bearing on the philosophy of time. Briefly, the trouble is apparently that we are no longer entitled to believe in an absolute " simultaneity " of events. There is no precise set of events throughout the universe all of which are simultaneous with one another, and before a subsequent set, and after a preceding set. From one point of view events A and B are contemporaneous, but from another (dependent on the movement of the observer) A may precede B ; and from yet another point of view B may precede A. Similarly, distances can no longer be regarded as absolute. And the two sets of variations, temporal and spatial, are interdependent and complementary, in such a manner as to suggest that time and space are in a sense (and only within narrow limits) convertible into one another. What appears from one point of view as an increase of time appears from another point of view as a decrease of space, and *vice versa.*

All this is very surprising, but we must hold fast to our concrete experience of time and space. In immediate experience the temporal aspect of events is qualitatively different from their spatial aspect. Time and space are " as different as chalk from cheese," nay much more different. Even if, in astronomical magnitudes they reveal a close interconnection, we must never be deluded into supposing that time is *merely* a fourth dimension of space.

On the other hand, it is quite conceivable that, to minds of a higher lucidity than ours, what appears to us as the temporal sequence of cosmical events may appear simultaneously " spread out " as a fourth spatial dimension, while a fifth dimension of events, wholly unknown to us, may constitute for those beings a genuine temporal dimension, in which events have passage.

It must be admitted that the impact of modern physics has made the past-present-future aspect of time seem less objective than of old. The universe certainly does consist of a vast system of spatio-temporal events related together in very complex and subtle manners. It is possible that the myriad " searchlights " of individual experiencing minds may travel in many different directions about the system, somewhat as in a four-handed game of Halma the four streams of individual pieces move across the board in four different directions. It is not inconceivable that some beings experience our physical universe " back to front," so that for them the law of entropy is reversed, and energy piles itself up into the stars.

But there is a difficulty in all these possibilities. They make nonsense of free choice. In ordinary life a man feels strongly that he *could* either do this or that. For instance, he *could* either plant an acorn in his garden or not. If he does, the universe may contain the career of a particular tree which would otherwise not exist. If freedom is real, the future cannot be pre-destined.

This consideration has made some philosophers believe that future events are non-existent in a sense in which past events are not non-existent. The past, they hold, is irrevocably what it is, and a part of reality. The present is the " growing-point " of the past. But the future is nothing at all until the course of events (including our own free choices) creates it.

It may be noted that such a view of time excludes pre-vision. If the future does not in any manner exist now, it is impossible to have access to it now. If our choos-ing *creates* one future rather than another, the future cannot be seen till it is brought into existence by choice.

If, on the other hand, we abandon the belief in arbi-trary free choice this difficulty does not arise. The system of events can then be regarded as fixed eternally. Our choices are therefore predestinate as factors in the system. They are free only in the sense that, and in so far as, they depend only on our own (determinate) nature, and not on the nature of something *other* than ourselves which compels us *against* our determinate will.

When we take into account all these conflicting con-siderations it is very clear that no satisfactory account of time can yet be given. Some aspects of temporal experience point emphatically toward the absolute reality of the " passage " of events, and therefore of the past-present-future distinction. Other aspects point no less emphatically toward equality of status for all spatio-temporal events. In these circumstances some philosophers simply dismiss " passage " as sheer illusion. Others merely ignore the difficulties and insist on its absolute reality.

In accord with my deliberate policy of facing both ways when neither aspect is exclusively satisfactory, I suggest that the most promising way of dealing with the problem is to cling to both sets of facts while frankly admitting that we cannot reconcile them. We may then express our view by saying that in *some* sense, not yet definable, passage is an objective character, and yet in *some* sense, not yet definable, events are *also* supra-temporal, or have an eternal aspect. To this statement we may add the surmise that perhaps the trouble lies much deeper than human philosophy can ever probe. It may be that human mentality itself, the half-developed mode of human immediate experience, does not reveal enough of the nature of time to permit of a logically coherent theory of it. Roughly this is the view of the Absolute Idealists; but they were sometimes inclined to go further and believe that time was *merely* subjective. This view, as we have seen, is unreasonable.

The conviction that our normal temporal experience, though it has access to an objective character of the universe, is also radically incomplete and incoherent, raises the question whether there is any positive evidence of any more penetrating kind of experience. It leads, in fact, to an intellectual assessment of the claims of the mystics.

III. MYSTICISM

Throughout this survey it has been borne in on us that intellectual knowledge, though reliable up to a point, is superficial, piecemeal, and sometimes treacherous; but hitherto we have barely noticed the claim that there is another kind of knowing which is penetrating, comprehensive, and infallible. I shall now briefly consider this claim as it is put forward by the mystics. European philosophy has been mainly intellectualistic in temper; Indian philosophy has been mainly mystical. The great European mystics have been moral leaders, but they have not been philosophers.

I shall consider mysticism only in the most general manner, and shall merely try to show what, in my view, is its relation to philosophy, which we have defined as the love and the pursuit of wisdom.

The word " mystical " is used in two very different senses. In the more general sense it applies to any ideas which are not strictly rational but have an element of intuitive guesswork in them. In this sense " mystical " sometimes becomes synonymous with " superstitious." In the stricter sense the word " mystical " applies to a special kind of non-rational experience, in which, it is claimed, the individual attains some degree of illumination or insight into the essential and normally hidden nature of reality. This insight is reported to be not merely a kind of knowing; it is the supreme achievement of knowing-feeling-striving in one all-fulfilling act. The " knowing " aspect of it is said to be not abstract, like intellectual knowing, but concrete, like sense-experience. In fact, in so far as it is knowledge, it is an immediate acquaintance with the hidden essence of a

414

" reality " which is said to lie behind all ordinary and illusory experience.

The reports of the mystics vary greatly, but in spite of their differences they show a remarkable agreement about the general character of the experience. I shall consider only the features which are most general.

The mystic's starting-point is often a condition of torturing self-contempt or of revulsion from the cruelty and injustice practised by his fellow men. It is important to recognise that his motives, like most human motives, are very complex. He certainly desires, amongst other things, personal salvation in some sense. Christians conceive this as eternal personal life, but some Indians reject this view. Another and a subtly entangled motive is spontaneous compassion and the desire for the spiritual fulfilment of others. Different from these motives is the self-oblivious admiration for virtue or for the spiritual way of living. In this mood the spiritual way of living is conceived not merely as a means to salvation but as an intrinsic good. Different again is the admiration or adoration or worship of a personal God, or of the universal Spirit, or of something quite indescribable save as the supremely holy object of worship. This may be conceived either in terms of love and tender intimacy or in terms of awe and even terror, or in both of these manners.

The aspirant to mystical experience is generally a highly self-conscious individual, and often highly other-conscious also. He seeks to escape from the bondage of the bodily hungers and of personal self-regard. And he seeks very often, but not always, to free others from this slavery. In Europe he is apt to say that he denies himself in order to save his soul, or find union

415

with his God. In the East he generally longs to annihilate his separate self and lose himself in the universal spirit.

Two different impulses appear among the mystics, often in the same individual. The first is the tendency to withdraw from the world in order to concentrate on self-discipline for the sake of the desired self-mastery and self-transcendence. The other is the tendency to play an active part in the world, to find his self-discipline in heroic social service, to find self-transcendence through absorption in the lives of others. It is claimed that the greatest mystics, at any rate in the West, have been not world-forsakers but world-embracers. In the East too, I understand, it is recognised that the final and most lethal temptation, the final snare of self, which traps many noble spirits when they are well on their way, is the temptation to shun all mundane responsibilities and seek self-annihilation for purely selfish motives.

Mastery over the flesh and the self-regarding passions is sought by various kinds of self-discipline. It often begins with special exercises to acquire voluntary control of bodily functions, such as breathing and blood-circulation. It may include fasting and other forms of asceticism, or actual " mortification of the flesh " by self-torture. It generally involves the religious exercises and ritual characteristic of the individual's social environment. Good works among his fellow men may also play a large part in it. It may take the form of meditation, in which the individual tries to concentrate his attention upon, or to yield himself in utter passivity to, the spiritualising influence of God, or of the Whole. Or he may seek by introspective meditation

416

to discover hidden imperfections in his own nature, so that he may eradicate them by spiritual discipline.

By such methods the mystics have sought their goal. Each method contains its own peculiar snares. Discipline of the flesh may turn into a perverse lust of self-torture or of spiteful cruelty to others. Every kind of self-denial may produce puritanical harshness. Good works may starve the inner life, and reduce the individual to a kind of charity-dealing robot. Meditation may lead to flight from social responsibility, and self-indulgence in a world of dreams; or to such a habit of self-analysis that the will is paralysed.

Amongst all these snares the traveller's progress is bound to be fluctuating and slow. Very different experiences are reported by different individuals, but the underlying identity is unmistakable. The story generally includes a phase, sometimes known as " the dark night of the soul," in which all contact with the universal seems to be lost, and the spirit sinks into despair. Subsequently the adventurer struggles out of this slough of despond to find himself nearer to his goal than he expected. Little by little he may gain complete detachment from all worldly desires and be able to meet every issue of fate not merely with stoical resignation but with joyful acceptance. For all things have now come to seem particular manifestations of the universal spirit in which he desires to lose himself.

The final illumination and self-transcendence are of course described very differently by mystics of Eastern and Western culture. All differences, it may be, are differences in the *interpretation* of experiences that are essentially identical and indescribable. Such, perhaps, is even the seemingly radical difference between those who claim union of the personal self with a personal deity and those who speak of the annihilation of the personal self in the impersonal Whole. We must bear in mind always that any experience that is beatific, and also too subtle for literal description, is likely to be interpreted in terms of the most cherished ideas of the individual's traditional culture. Consequently, in Christian lands and ages it is almost inevitable that interpretation should conform to the ideals of personal immortality and union with a personal God.

In general the ecstatic experience, which is the mystic's supreme reward, is said to give profound insight into the essential nature of reality, along with a stammering inability to describe *what* has been revealed, save in the most metaphorical and paradoxical terms. Sometimes the reality thus revealed is referred to in terms of dread, and even terror, as the divine and ruthless " Other," rightly careless of man and his petty desires. In some cultures, on the other hand, it is said to be the divine, personified Love, which embraces, or gathers up into itself, the spirit of the individual lover of this all-loving God. In other cultures it appears as the impersonal and wholly dispassionate universal spirit, or the underlying reality which constitutes the unity of all things. One point on which there is general agreement is that in the supreme experience time is in some sense transcended. What is discovered is a reality which is eternal.

The effect of mystical experiences on the individual's ordinary life is claimed to be far-reaching. All his conduct is irradiated by memory of his vision. He is able to surmount all troubles with fortitude and joy. He behaves with increased wisdom, sincerity, courage, and devotion to whatever social ideal he has espoused.

He is spurred by a new sense of the reality that informs all ordinary phenomenal things. Even sense-perception may reveal unexpected significance to him, significance of the essential nature of the universe. He has an immensely increased capacity for delighting in everything. In particular he may discover an intrinsic worth and lovableness in his fellow human beings, even in those who, in their blindness, pursue evil ends. In short, he becomes a much more sensitive, more practical, more alert, more integrated, more genuinely social personality. Such is the claim.

It is easy to dismiss these contentions as mere delusion. It is easy to point out that alcohol, nitrous-oxide, opium and other drugs may induce ecstatic moods and beatific visions remarkably like some aspects of mystical experience. Simple starvation also may cause a striking mental lucidity and exaltation. Most remarkable is the well-attested fact that the onset of an epileptic attack may be accompanied by a conviction of profound insight and beatitude. Such evidence suggests that the mystic merely deludes himself into " projecting " upon the external universe a sense of extreme personal well-being which has been caused in him by nothing more exalted than glandular action in his own body.

Another argument against the objective validity of mystical experience may be derived from modern psychology. It is obvious that the language in which some mystics describe their experience is tinged with sexual metaphor. This vaunted union with the divine may after all be merely a hallucination bred of suppressed sexual craving. Or alternatively it may be a grandiose expression of primitive self-regard, or of the infantile longing for parental care, or for return to the womb, and annihilation.

The cogency of all such arguments is immensely enhanced by the contemporary disposition to regard explanations in terms of scientific concepts as more credible than any other. We have already noted that the supposed metaphysical implications of science are based on the hypostatisation of the physical categories and the dismissal of all others as unreal. But though we must discount this prejudice in favour of the physical, we must not rush to the other extreme of accepting the mystic's claims uncritically. We must consider whether they can in fact be properly accounted for in terms of familiar concepts. What then must our judgment be ? What is the reasonable verdict from the point of view of the plain man who has not himself had any mystical experience ?

The mystic can account for the physically-induced seemingly mystical experiences by arguing that *of course* there is a physical aspect to the process of mastering the flesh, and that some of the phenomena produced during self-discipline may also be produced by purely physical causes. He may go further, and say that these physically-induced experiences really are approximations to the authentic mystical experience, though so oddly caused. In fact, if he has already made up his mind about the validity of mystical experience, he need not be disturbed by the arguments derived from physiology, nor yet by those derived from psychology.

But *ought* he to have made up his mind ? Or rather, ought we, who do not share his experience, to accept his verdict ? The main facts to remember are : that a large number of persons in all countries and all ages have claimed mystical experience ; that in spite of diversity their reports show on the whole a surprising agreement; that many of them, though certainly not all, have been persons well above the average of intelligence and integrity; that some of them are the world's greatest saints, moral teachers, religious and socially dynamic leaders; that among ordinary people in most phases of the world's history, though not in our own, the belief in, and the very fragmentary apprehension of, some kind of mystical reality has been a source of strength. It is true, of course, that, like other good things, mystical experience may become a snare. It may be used as an occasion for flight from the responsibilities of this life. Undoubtedly this has often happened. But such withdrawal is emphatically condemned by some of the greatest mystics. It is possible that it occurs only in individuals and in cultural phases of somewhat depressed spiritual vigour.

In view of all these considerations it seems rash to accept the simple materialistic theory that all mystical experience is merely an illusion. It seems on the whole probable that the mystics do have access of some kind to something which is missed in ordinary experience, and may have a supremely invigorating effect on the individual, and therefore on his behaviour.

On the other hand, all intellectual descriptions and interpretations of the mystical experience must be regarded with great suspicion. It is after all very unlikely that human thought and language, which are adapted to much simpler, more commonplace experience, should be able to cope with experience of a very different order. Descriptions and interpretations can be intelligible only to those who have at least some slight immediate acquaintance with the matters described.

The plain man may reasonably feel that this conclusion is both vague and unconvincing. He may say, " You *may* be right. But the whole thing *may* be moonshine. I have no personal knowledge of any such experience, and I shall continue to regard the mystic's claims with grave suspicion."

But *has* he no personal acquaintance with mystical experience of any kind ? Have not very many fairly sensitive people some acquaintance at least with a mystical aspect of normal experience ? In our materialistically-obsessed civilisation it is difficult for them to recognise the fact. Perhaps many who have it overlook it. There are many kinds of normal experience which to the sincerely observing mind do *seem* to reveal an aspect which deserves the name mystical. In these experiences some particular fact is strongly felt to be in some incomprehensible manner significant of the essential nature of the universe. The most obvious example of this kind of experience is perhaps youthful falling in love. Sometimes, but not always, the lover feels very strongly that either love itself or the nature of the loved person gives him a new and penetrating insight. It is easy to dismiss this seemingly mystical aspect as merely a product of uncritical emotion. It is always fatally easy to dismiss unobtrusive facts that do not accord with our theories. Another kind of experience which may have a mystical flavour is the appreciation of " natural beauty," as Wordsworth knew. Less obviously, and less frequently, intellectual exploration may give the same impression, when matters which were obscure suddenly assume a far-reaching pattern. Artistic creation and appreciation are often felt to have a mystical aspect over and above their normal æsthetic character. Most strikingly this is revealed in tragic art. In watching a great play, in which the leading characters present themselves both as unique individuals and as symbols of humanity striving to mould its destiny, we are torn between human sympathy for the individual and acceptance of his tragic fate. The experience is not purely æsthetic; or if it is, then the æsthetic itself has a mystical aspect. We feel that in some obscure way the tissue of fictitious events symbolises a terrible and yet somehow a *right* characteristic of the universe. It is too easy (to repeat) to explain away this aspect of tragedy, in terms, let us say, of suppressed sadism or some other unwitting craving.

Perhaps the most impressive of all the ways in which the normal person may sometimes gain a hint of mystical experience is in grave personal danger or pain, or distress of any kind, and even in the agony of pity for one who is loved and is suffering. On such occasions one may find oneself strangely divided. The normal self is strained almost to breaking-point by unbearable terror or pain or compassion; and yet, even in the case of compassion, one sees the dread event as a revealing symbol of reality, and as such one accepts it, not merely with resignation but with a sense that even this is involved in the terrible but somehow *right* nature of the universe. And so, even while one is perhaps behaving with panic terror or horror, one is also, in some strange manner, fundamentally peaceful and glad.

I suggest the following tentative conclusion about this whole subject. In mystical experience, of all sorts from the humblest to the most exalted, the human mind gropingly reaches out to a mode of apprehension very different from all " normal " experience. This kind of apprehension is attained confusedly and precariously by quite a large number of people in the course of normal experiences, though it is seldom recognised as such. A very small number, whose mental development reaches to the extreme limit of human capacity, enjoy a much fuller measure of it, and can know it with much greater clarity and assurance. I suggest further that mystical experience is both one of the most dangerous moral snares and one of the most important sources of moral strength, not only for those who go far in it but also for all normally sensitive and intelligent persons.

But what of the philosophy of mystical experience ? How are we to think of it ? Is it really a kind of *knowledge*, a peculiar insight into hidden reality ? We may perhaps more truly think of it in a somewhat different manner. In every kind of mystical experience, from that most closely associated with normal experience to that which is described by the great mystics, there occurs some kind of self-discipline and some kind of consequent vision. But the vision, I should say, is not most satisfactorily described as a discovery of hidden reality ; it is rather a discovery of a new kind of value or worth or excellence or beauty in the normally experienced world. This *rightness* (we have no more satisfactory word) was formerly overlooked, and now suddenly confronts the mind. In fact, mystical experience constitutes essentially a new and more awakened way of *feeling about* the world. But " feeling about " must not be taken to mean a purely subjective attitude. It must mean a subjective attitude which is *appropriate*, objectively justified by, the real nature of the universe in relation to the real nature of the individual mind.

In this theory of mystical experience there is a very serious difficulty. How can the mystical attitude of delighted acceptance of the universe as perfect be reconciled with the moral attitude which distinguishes between good and bad, right and wrong, and recognises an obligation to struggle for the good against the bad, seeking thus to improve a universe which is regarded as very far from perfect? Plainly there is a logical conflict here, and it is useless to pretend that there is not.

I have argued that moral right and wrong depend on the intuited goodness of the free activity of conscious beings, and particularly on the fulfilling of personality-in-community. It almost seems as though the mystic, and the plain man in his rare half-mystical apprehension, had access to another kind of " good," independent of conscious beings, a " good " which somehow embraced ordinary good and evil, right and wrong. This view, it must be admitted, is both unintelligible and dangerous. It is dangerous because it may lead to a complacent acquiescence in the misfortunes of others, as being " all in the picture," all needed for the perfection of the universe.

On the other hand, it is undoubtedly a psychological fact that, in spite of the seeming logical inconsistency, mystical experience does very often clarify the moral consciousness and strengthen moral behaviour. Gautama Buddha, Socrates, Jesus Christ, Mohammed, and, I believe, Spinoza are outstanding examples. It is not impossible that Lenin too, though he would have been indignant at the suggestion, owed his strength partly to unrecognised mystical experience.

It may be that at the human level of mental development a satisfactory intellectual solution of this conflict between moral protest and mystical acceptance is impossible. But we may grope toward a solution in the following manner. We may regard the human mind as having two aspects. In the one aspect a man is a finite individual; and his concern, his whole duty, is to champion the cause of personality-in-community in the human world. And this human enterprise is probably one minor theme in the universal enterprise of the advancement of the spirit through personality-in-community in a host of worlds. It may be that at some date in the history of the cosmos this enterprise will be fulfilled in the attainment of the perfection of knowing-feeling-striving through the experience of some cosmical society of worlds. Or perhaps this is too trite a way of conceiving the culmination of the cosmical process. Perhaps the spiritual perfection of the cosmos as a whole involves no such triumph of the enterprise of finite minds, but rather their partial defeat, much as the well-being of a living organism involves all sorts of internal, intra-organic conflicts, strains, and partial defeats. Of this we know nothing. But clearly the human individual in one of his aspects feels called to play a minute part in the great widespread struggle for personality-in-community.

Let us suppose, however, that he has also another aspect, in which he finds precarious contact with the eternal and perfected spirit of the cosmos, and in which his will tends to conform to that spirit, in the sense that he is no longer enslaved to the cravings of the separate self, or even to the service of the ideal of personality-in-community, but is able, so to speak, haltingly to feel all things from the universal point of view. In this mode of experience he recognises intuitively that the cosmos *is* an overwhelmingly glorious thing, and that all the struggle and defeat and agony of finite minds, no less than their partial triumph, are justified by the perfection of the whole. He realises that it is foolish and impious to demand that the universe shall be moral, or that the universal spirit shall be moral, or that " God " shall be good. These, he feels, do not exist for the sake of morality. On the contrary, morality exists for them.

In some such manner we may try to cope with the seeming logical conflict between the two fundamental religious experiences : between the moral protest, which seeks to alter the universe, and the ecstatic acceptance of the universe, with all its glory and its shame, its joy and its distress, its beauty, and all its squalor.

But if this intellectual reconciliation is unsound, which it may well be, let us never forget that these two experiences do in fact support one another, and that for the wise conduct of practical life both are needed.

CHAPTER XIII

THE PRACTICAL UPSHOT

WHAT is the practical upshot of our whole enquiry ? How should it influence us in private and in public action ?

To answer this question, we must first take note of the most significant features of our civilisation to-day. Some are obvious. One, and that perhaps the most important of all, is easily overlooked. It is obvious that science is transforming the life of the whole race. It is obvious that the East is destined to play a far more active part than it has done hitherto. It is obvious to all who are fairly intelligent and informed, and not blinded by some special disability, that Western civilisation is being undermined by vested economic interests and by absolute national sovereignty. It is fairly obvious that the issue of the present world-wide confusion must be either chaos and degeneration or a world in which the means of production are in some effective manner communally controlled. It is obvious that the forces of reaction are at present relatively hopeful and resolute, while the forces of progress are for the moment disunited, bewildered, and irresolute.

What is not so obvious is that a sinister change of temper is spreading throughout the civilised world and threatening to destroy both the flower and the root of civilisation. As the years pass we are tending more and more to abandon the two principles which constitute at once the goal and the essential means of civilised living. We are losing faith in the free critical intelligence. And we are losing faith in charity.

To understand the importance of this change, let us remember how our species triumphed. Throughout man's career intelligence and charity have been man's distinctive and most valuable assets. One of our early pre-human ancestors is said to have been much like the Spectral Tarsier, a little mammal about the size of a mouse, with long wiry fingers and huge forward-looking eyes adapted for binocular vision. Not by weapons but by correlation of subtle eyes and subtle hands through subtle brain, this creature triumphed. And man himself conquered the world by the same means, by attention, by discrimination, by skilled manipulation, by versatility; in fact by intelligence and imagination in adapting himself to an ever-changing environment.

But intelligence and imagination have not been his sole outfit. By means of these he developed a more precise and penetrating kind of awareness of himself and others than is possible to sub-human animals. At some stage or other men began to be conscious of themselves and their fellows as conscious agents, having distinctive characters and needs. This new power enabled them gradually to attain, though rarely and precariously, a new kind of social experience and social behaviour. Sociality, as we have seen, is of two types: the distinctively animal and the distinctively human; that which demands only herd-mentality, and that which demands also the capacity for true community, based on the mutual respect of self-conscious and other-conscious individuals.

These then, the critical and imaginative intelligence

and the capacity for community, are the powers by which man has risen. Both of them, particularly the latter, are fragmentary and precarious; but both have until recently been regarded as essential to civilisation. The tragedy of our time lies in the fact that, besides declining in scope, they are actually coming into disrepute.

In the Victorian age it seemed that the future lay with Liberalism, if by that name we may refer not merely to a political policy but to an attitude of mind, a culture, which was accepted by most men, irrespective of party. This attitude of mind had been conceived by, and was appropriate to, the needs of the rising bourgeois class in its fight for independence against the feudal aristocracy. Along with some distorted ideas that were special to the circumstances of the bourgeois class, Liberalism included two perennially important principles, namely, faith in the free intelligence, and respect for human individuality. All other liberal principles, good and bad, were derived from these. Economic *laissez faire*, the freedom of the individual to buy in the cheapest market and sell in the dearest; political democracy, the freedom of the individual to take a share in the control of public policy by voting; freedom of conscience; freedom from superstition; freedom of expression; freedom of physical and mental growth through universal comfort and security and universal education—these ideals, which were accepted by very many intelligent citizens, were thought to be capable of speedy realisation throughout the civilised world. Not only so, but the " scientific spirit," the new temper of disinterested enquiry which had been so painfully acquired during the preceding three centuries, and had

431

become associated with Liberalism, seemed at last to be coming into its own.

These expectations, as we have already noted, turned out to be false. Liberalism failed to fulfil its promise. Its failure was due partly to the fact that it stressed individuality at the expense of community, partly to the insincerity with which its principles were applied in practice, partly to the general reaction from intellectualism.

The root of the trouble, as we have seen, was that the policy of *laissez faire* was not implemented with equality of bargaining power. It favoured fortunate individuals at the expense of society. It brought not the millennium but plutocracy and wage-slavery. It brought the rivalry of industrial empires competing for the exploitation of backward lands and peoples. It brought also, though against its will, tariff walls and neurotic patriotism, arming to the teeth. Indirectly, and in spite of itself, it brought the European War.

What followed ? The war accustomed men to discipline and to conformity. The exigencies of war, abroad and at home, and the exigencies of class-domination, tightened discipline in every sphere. Not only the Liberal Party, but the far more widespread Liberal mentality, was torn by an internal conflict, a conflict between democratic ideals and the expediency of defending the social order which it, the bourgeois class, controlled. Liberal principles suited a rising but not a dominant class.

Meanwhile, among the workers not individualism but collective action against the employers had proved the only remedy against oppression. This fact discredited the whole system of Liberal ideas, both the good and the bad. It was from Russia that Liberalism received its death-blow. There the tendency to sink the individual in the militant party and class gained immense prestige from the success of the Revolution and the founding of a social order planned in the workers' interests.

In Italy and Germany the same disgust with individualism brought the same tendency to energise and discipline the individual by persuading him to regard himself merely as a member of a group. But here the issue was a very different social order.

In the reaction from Liberalism we must distinguish two opposed but closely entangled factors, namely, an advance toward the will for genuine community and a regression toward the herd-mentality. In Russia, Italy, and Germany there has been a revulsion from individualism; and both the herd-mentality and the will for community have played a great part. It seems probable, however, that while in Russia the will for community has, on the whole, been dominant, in Italy and Germany the main factor has been herd-mentality, stimulated and used for private ends by individualistic capitalists and social adventurers.

The decline of Liberalism as a social policy brought with it the decline of Liberalism as a cultural ideal. In the more industrialised lands this cultural change was accentuated by a growing emotional revulsion from " scientific materialism," which was closely associated with Liberalism.

This change of feeling had two aspects. In general it was a reaction against the extravagant claims of the champions of the abstract intellect, in fact against a narrow intellectualism; and it was a particular protest against the intellectual undermining of morality. The belief that mind was a meaningless accident in the universe, and that moral values were merely subjective, seemed to be involved in the scientific world-view. This abstraction and hypostatisation of physical qualities was unjustified, but it accorded with the general preoccupation with the commercial aspect of the material world. Materialism, however, doubtless supported by a craving to be rid of tiresome moral obligations, led to the overthrow of the old moral sanctions. This revolution produced, particularly in the " advanced circles " of capitalistic countries, an irresponsible, sordid, and despair-racked way of life. This, or the reaction which it caused in spectators, gave rise in time to a phase of widespread disgust and horror at the effects of moral nihilism. The emotional tide turned once more toward self-discipline and even toward a " mystical " sanction for morality in some kind of religious devotion.

But devotion to what? The old religion had lost its power. A new one was urgently needed.

In one country alone this need was not seriously felt, or at least not recognised. Soviet Russia had not suffered from the disillusionment and degeneracy of Western Europe. In Russia, society itself, in the form of the proletarian State, became the supreme object of veneration. And dialectical materialism strangely assumed much of the glamour of a mystical religion.

But in Italy and Germany materialism was blamed for social degeneracy. The deep need for a mystical sanction for values gave birth to the fantastic mythology of the divine race. The racial myth is based on the biologically unsound notion that the cultural differences between peoples are caused mainly by differences of biological stock, and that some races are innately nobler than others. This false conception is given an emotional appeal by the vague and wholly unfounded belief that one's own race is the best of all, and moreover has been entrusted with a divine mission to rule the world, or is itself an embodiment of the divine principle.

It is perhaps well to say in passing that, though we must emphatically condemn the culture which at present dominates Italy and Germany, it would be folly on our part to indulge in self-righteous censure of these great peoples themselves. The social neurosis which has seized them was bred of agony and dire frustration. And these were caused partly by cruel treatment at the hands of more fortunate neighbours, partly by the tragic failure of Liberalism.

The triumph of Liberalism had depended on the free exercise of the critical intelligence. Its downfall brought the free intelligence into contempt. In Russia, no doubt, intelligence is still prized; but it is muzzled and only allowed to function in directions approved by the State. Moreover, the discovery that all thought is unwittingly biassed has given rise, not only in Russia, to the perverse and lethal notion that distortion of facts and arguments is praiseworthy so long as it inclines in directions favourable to the social ideals of the thinker.

. In Italy and Germany the free intelligence has been much more severely persecuted. The finer brains of both countries have been either exiled or destroyed. In the schools the young are brought up to believe that criticism of the official ideology is always misleading and wicked. If the present regime continues, these two great peoples may within a generation suffer a very serious all-round reduction of mental capacity. Communists explain the Fascist annihilation of culture as a necessary result of the necessary hostility of capitalism to the free intelligence which tends to expose its weakness. No doubt there is much truth in this view. We must not forget, however, that in Russia also there is ruthless oppression and restriction of free criticism. This is officially attributed to the need for unity against threatened attack from within and without. It is true that grave danger inevitably brings oppression and cultural decline, and that in every country to-day insecurity, frustration, and fear are in fact producing this result. But it is difficult not to be gravely perturbed by recurrent shootings in Russia.

Liberalism was associated not only with the free exercise of intelligence but with a morality based on human brotherhood. This was a legacy from Christianity. It did not logically fit into the materialistic and ethically sceptical metaphysics that science had bred, but it accorded with the Liberal respect for individuality. Even within the sphere of Liberalism, however, it could not have long survived. We have already noticed the widespread " taboo on tenderness " that seized Western culture under the influence of science. A much more violent rejection of the orthodox tenderness-morality occurred in Italy and Germany as part of the emotional reaction against Liberalism. In fact, combined with a protest against ethical scepticism and moral licentiousness, there was a protest against the particular kind of morality which had for so long inspired Liberalism at its best. As against materialism, Fascism has reinstated morality, but as against Christianity it has dethroned love and set in its place courage and ruthless mastery. Finally, it is perhaps worth while to remark that, just as the racial myth necessitates suppression of the free intelligence that ridicules it, so this harsh morality demands a gradual blunting of all the finer sensibilities that condemn it.

It must not be supposed that the democratic countries (so-called) have been exempt from these tendencies. In Britain, for instance, what do we find ? The key to the understanding of the whole process lies in the fact that the capitalistic social order is faced with very grave difficulties. In times of prosperity the owning class, influenced by Liberalism and spurred by the demands of the workers, tended to become comparatively tolerant and paternal. But recurrent financial crises, the fear of social disorder, and the necessity to arm extravagantly for the maintenance of imperial economic privileges are producing a very different temper. Already there are signs that tolerance and paternalism are giving way to a harsher spirit. This is partly the result of the inevitable increase of industrial centralisation. The individual firms of each industry tend to collaborate to restrict output and maintain prices. Capitalistic private enterprise is voluntarily controlling free competition in order to preserve the system. As yet there is no grand co-ordination of all industries, but it will come. At present, Parliament tries ineffectively to arbitrate between them. In time, presumably, the industries themselves will establish a central co-ordinating body, a sort of Fascist Grand Council.

Meanwhile, the tendency to Fascism is plain in other respects. Democracy is discredited by the supine behaviour of Parliamentary Governments. At the same time we see a steady encroachment on civil liberties. Police powers are extended. Attempts are made to discipline the people through gas-drills, and perhaps through the otherwise very desirable physical culture movement. Approval is given to hooligan action against persons whose political opinions are disliked. Conscription is in the air. Increasingly the press, the radio, and the cinema become sensitive to Government suggestions for suppression or " interpretation " of facts. Along with all this we must note a change of moral temper, a slow but steady drift away from the tenderness morality of Liberalism and Christianity. Amongst intellectuals of a certain type we find, for instance, a disposition to defend blood-sports, including bull-fighting. There are signs that approval of corporal punishment is increasing, along with morbid delight in the infliction of it. Everywhere we encounter the first symptoms of the movement from kindliness to " firmness."

It appears, then, that not only in the Fascist countries, and not only in these and Russia, but also in the " Democracies," there is a steady flight from the principles of Liberalism, both good and bad. I suggest that this cultural change is at bottom a consequence of the economic forces at work in our day. In fact I suggest that economic determinism is thrusting us not toward the Marxian Utopia but toward Fascism; and that, if economic determinism cannot be restrained, we are doomed.

The Marxian believes that this tendency toward Fascism occurs only in capitalist countries, and that sooner or later capitalism will crack, and the proletariat will seize control. He grossly underestimates the powers of propaganda and coercion in the hands of the owning class, and the gullibility of the masses. Also he underestimates, or still worse excuses as a temporary expedient, the tendency toward Fascism in Russia. It is necessary to face the possibility that the Communist party in Russia, in spite of its magnificent record of devotion, may ultimately degenerate into an oppressive bureaucracy or a reactionary religious hierarchy. May this fear prove unfounded !

Is there any hope of checking this trend of economic determinism ? I believe that there is, though only a forlorn one. But forlorn hopes sometimes kindle the best in human nature and carry it to miraculous triumph. The only hope, I suggest, is that there may be a wide-spread and emphatic assertion of the will for true community. If, as I have argued, there was something more than economic determinism (in the narrow sense) in Early Christianity, in the French Revolution, and in the Russian Revolution itself, something without which these great events could never have been achieved, then there is after all a hope that the same spirit may yet refashion the whole world.

This spirit, however it has been described in the past, has always manifested two aspects, which in modern idiom consist of faith in the free intelligence and will for true community.

If this is correct, then the practical upshot of our survey of philosophy is obvious. Our main theoretical conclusion has been an increased reliance on the validity of the dispassionate intelligence and on the ideal of personality-in-community. If, as I have argued, philosophy does not end with theory, but is the love and the pursuit of wisdom, this conclusion must not remain purely theoretical. We have seen that in the contemporary world the dispassionate intelligence and the spirit of true community are falling into disrepute, and that their decline threatens to bring the human race to grave disaster. Clearly, then, the practical effect of our survey must be to stimulate us to do our utmost both in private life and in public life to foster these two essential factors in civilisation.

But though the free intelligence and the spirit of community are, I believe, by far the most important influences for civilising the world, we must not suppose that as abstract principles they constitute by themselves a panacea for all our troubles. To say, as some do, that if only we will be constant to these principles all will be well, is not enough. They are *all*-sufficient only when they are almost universally accepted, and accepted with sincere conviction. In the present world there is no prospect that this will soon be the case. On the contrary, even lip-service to them is dwindling; and at the best of times only a small minority will be capable of practising them constantly and sincerely.

Moreover, public events since the European War have shown all too grimly that a vague inclination toward sincere thinking and kindly behaviour is utterly powerless against a ruthless adventurer or a ruthless class, armed with modern weapons of propaganda and coercion. In our disjointed world there are too many dangerous neurotics who cannot be speedily turned from destructiveness by reasonable persuasion or by the power of non-violence. In the long run, assuredly, reason and love will prevail. And even to-day they are by far the most important instruments of civilisation.

But unaided they cannot deal successfully with every crisis that threatens us with a further incursion of the new barbarism. We must face the fact that, though the free intelligence and the spirit of community are at once the goal and an essential means, they may be not only ineffectual but actually harmful, unless they are combined with a full measure of that hot indignation against tyranny, that devoted service in the struggle for the new order, which is characteristic of the best minds of the political Left.

On the other hand, the political Left, if it is to capture the imagination and allegiance of the people of this country and sweep them forward to victory, must, I believe, learn a more liberal spirit. I mean, of course, liberal not in the political but in the cultural sense, namely, loyalty to the free critical intelligence and respect for the human individual. For how do things stand ? Up and down the country, up and down the world, in every class and every political party, outside the churches and inside them, there are increasing numbers of well-disposed and sensible men and women who are ready to make real sacrifices if thereby they can help to create a better social order and a peace that shall be lasting and world-wide. Many of those who have social and economic privileges are beginning to realise that such privileges are both unjust and doomed to vanish. Not only so, but many, in all social classes, who are citizens of capitalistic states with imperial privileges, are reluctantly beginning to see that their far-reaching advantages over less-favoured peoples are equally unjust and unmaintainable. Perhaps in time they will become reconciled to surrendering them.

But this growing mass of well-meaning bewildered

public opinion is ineffective. One of the main reasons of its futility lies in the fact that no political party fully deserves its trust. The Conservatives are blinded by the prejudices of capitalism. The Liberals are often equally so. Labour is paralysed by the incubus of trade-union leadership. The Communists, unique in devotion and courage, have gained a reputation for impracticable and doctrinaire policies and for political ineptitude. Moreover, the rank and file of the Communist party, and all but the best of its leaders, are too apt to play into their opponents' hands by indulging in a very excusable but none the less impolitic extravagance and bitterness.

Yet the increasing mass of politically waking people might, I believe, be brought whole-heartedly to support the Left and to make real sacrifices, if they could be sure that the Left was inspired, not only by righteous indignation and the will for a new social order, but also by outstanding intellectual integrity and respect for human individuality. Rightly or wrongly, people are afraid of Communism for the same reasons as they are afraid of Fascism. They are afraid that if it came into power it would prove more tyrannical than the present order, that it would regiment people intolerably and suppress criticism with much the same ruthlessness as Fascism. No doubt this impression is partly a result of hostile propaganda, but not entirely so.

The most urgent task of the Left to-day is to convince the mass of politically waking members of all classes that it stands not for a new kind of oppression and a new kind of censorship but for human kindliness and for the free intelligence. If the vague and confused forces of good will in this country and in the world are to be brought together to form a really effective movement for radical social change and world change, they must not only be taught true theories and sound policies; they must also find both a philosophy and a religion. And for this end the leaders of this great movement, which is so slowly and so tardily coming into being, must manifestly appear to be not only astute politicians, not only wise statesmen, but moral leaders. They must have the very highest degree of personal integrity. And by personal integrity I mean not merely incorruptibility in the face of personal temptations; for this is, or should be, a commonplace political virtue. I mean far more than this, namely that these champions of a new world must be relied on to preserve through all the excitements and emergencies of political action their fundamental loyalty to the ideal of personality-in-community and their respect for the free critical intelligence. I mean that they must be manifestly incapable of seeking any speedy but superficial triumph for the cause by means which in the long run will frustrate the achievement of the true social aim.

Apart from obvious economic ills, what is most wrong with the world to-day is that we have lost faith in the distinctively human attributes of man, namely, the free critical intelligence and the capacity for mutual respect. Leaders who combine sound social policies with unshakable and unmistakable loyalty to these principles will be able to inspire us, not only with a reluctant acceptance of the need to take serious risks, but with the will to follow such leaders constantly, even, if necessary, through the gravest sacrifices, in the faith that they are true builders of the new world.

APPENDIX

SUGGESTIONS FOR READING PHILOSOPHY

(a) *The Approach.*—When I was adolescent, and beginning to worry about myself and the universe, I was encouraged to read popular books on scientific subjects. I was not encouraged to read philosophy. In spite of the fact that my education in science had been very slight, since I was made to concentrate on " English " subjects, I managed to glean in this way quite a lot of significant morsels of scientific knowledge, and to concoct a fairly nutritive mental diet for the growing mind. But though my " philosophy of life " seemed to me coherent, it was in fact very confused. I had no idea that the metaphysical assumptions of popular scientific culture needed to be brought to light and severely criticised. For I was discouraged from reading philosophy. But though I did not read philosophy I came in time to realise that there was in fact a great continent of thought which I had never explored. It was a continent which was at once enticing, forbidden, and forbidding. Whenever, with guilt, and with greed for mental gold, I dared to set foot upon its coast, I found myself at once faced with a dense jungle of technicalities and obscure ideas which, if they were not nonsense, were far beyond my comprehension. My young and ill-equipped mind had no means of penetrating into the hinterland. In disheartenment I fled back to the familiar continent of science, where the outposts of scientific culture were rapidly spreading across the still undeveloped areas in a kind of " ribbon development."

Since those days many useful books have been written to help the novice in philosophy. I propose to make a few suggestions both as to the best way of using this introductory material, and as to somewhat more advanced reading in philosophy. Much depends, of course, on the individual's special temperament and circumstances. Those who have a real gift for philosophical thinking will " lap up " books which others regard as almost unreadable. Those who have plenty of time at their disposal can

445

embark on a thorough and far-reaching campaign. Those who have little leisure need to plan their reading so as to secure a maximum result from as few books as possible. Again, some will approach philosophy through some particular subject in which they have come up against philosophical problems. Thus physical science, biology, psychology, art, religion, political aims, may for different kinds of people provide the incentive to philosophical study, first in the particular sphere of these interests, but later in all other philosophical fields. Some explorers, however, will want to begin with a more general approach. It is mainly for these that this book has been written, and for these that I append the following notes on reading.

I do so with grave hesitation, because, owing to an excessively late start, my own study of philosophy has been hasty and incomplete. Moreover, recently it has come almost to a standstill. I look forward with some apprehension to the comments of the thoroughly trained academic philosopher, toward whom I feel the respect due from the amateur to the professional. It is all too likely that my survey of philosophical literature for beginners ignores some important works, and gives a mistaken estimate of others. All that I can claim is that my list embraces many books that I myself have found helpful, and one or two that I now recognise as important though I have not yet read them.

For another reason also I hesitate to advise people about reading philosophy, namely, that I have so seldom taken such advice myself. Instead of holding to a well-planned course of study, I have nearly always inclined to " seize every hour, sip every flower." And whether or not it can be truly said of me that, like the sparrow, I " at all times was ready for love," it can certainly be said that at all times I was ready for philosophy. This readiness, in season and out of season, for philosophical discussion, reading, or thinking is one of the essential prerequisites for serious philosophical enquiry of any kind. The other is, of course, a tolerably keen intelligence. But I hasten to assure readers that, just as Einstein could be a great mathematician although he could not (according to the story) count his change, so it is possible to be fairly intelligent in philosophy even though one may be incompetent in some other spheres.

To sum the matter, I advise readers not to take my advice too seriously. With these words of caution I proceed.

(b) *General Introductions.*—It would be a great mistake to begin by reading nothing but introductions, but some sort of map of the country to be explored, or at any rate some clear point of departure, is desirable at the outset. There are two kinds of introduction to philosophy. One is the development of one problem so as to show that it involves other problems. The other kind is a general summary of all problems. Starting with an introduction of one or the other type, the intelligent reader will probably find his interest concentrating on some particular set of problems raised, and will want to pursue that theme with all possible thoroughness. He may, for instance, specialise in the philosophy of science or in social philosophy. But first let him try one or other of the following introductions.

Bertrand Russell's *The Problems of Philosophy* (Home University Library), published in 1912, and many times reprinted, is a brilliant introduction which starts with the question whether we have any certain knowledge of anything. It is a small volume, but in it the author, one of the outstanding philosophers of our age, states with his accustomed lucidity the core of several modern philosophical problems, such as the status of the external world, the nature of knowledge, the status of universals. The reader should be warned that Russell subsequently modified in important respects the principles laid down in this book. In all his works he favours philosophical Realism, but his characteristic development of it as " Neutral Monism " occurred after he wrote this Introduction. Another very valuable introduction, also Realist in general tenor, but more comprehensive than Russell's little book, is C. E. M. Joad's *Guide to Philosophy.* Readers will find that I have made use of Joad's treatment of several subjects. He has a surprising gift for expounding difficult ideas in such a manner that we are left wondering why people say philosophy is obscure. His much slighter *Introduction to Modern Philosophy* summarises Realism, recent Idealism, Pragmatism, and Bergson's views.

Of the second type of introduction, G. Watts-Cunningham's *Problems of Philosophy* is a useful introductory summary of opposing theories in all the great fields of philosophical study.

It is far less stimulating than the introductions by Russell and Joad, but is useful as a textbook or book of reference.

It is impossible to understand modern philosophy without understanding how it arose out of the philosophy of previous ages.

Clement C. J. Webb's *History of Philosophy* (Home University Library) may be strongly recommended. It deals very briefly and clearly with the whole sequence of philosophical thought from Ancient Greece to the Nineteenth Century. The author's own philosophical position is Idealist. A more advanced and very useful textbook is A. K. Rogers's *A Student's History of Philosophy*. Once more the general temper is Idealist. Will Durant's *The Story of Philosophy*, a much larger volume, is a bright and typically American account of the lives and theories of all the outstanding philosophers of Europe and America.

John Laird's *Recent Philosophy* (Home University Library) is a brief survey of philosophical movements in the present century. It presupposes some knowledge of philosophy. For Greek philosophy, Joad's *Guide* contains chapters on the metaphysical thought of Plato and Aristotle. For those who wish to concentrate on ancient philosophy, John Burnet's *Early Greek Philosophy* is the standard survey. G. C. Field's *Plato and his Contemporaries* is of great interest to readers who wish to pursue this theme.

(c) *General Development of Modern Philosophy.*—In whatever field the reader wishes to specialise he must make himself acquainted with the main works of the great philosophers of the last three centuries. All modern thought is a development of their thought, and is not fully intelligible without some first-hand knowledge of their work. In this connection the reader will find particularly useful the little philosophical volumes in The Modern Student's Library (Scribners). Each of these consists of carefully selected passages from one of the great philosophers and an introduction by an eminent authority. The list of volumes comprises Plato, Aristotle, Bacon, Descartes, Locke, Berkeley, Hume, Kant, Hegel, and Schopenhauer. There are also two volumes on Mediæval Philosophy. Very useful philosophical volumes occur also in Everyman's Library. Most of them have helpful introductions by A. D. Lindsay.

For practical purposes modern philosophy may be said to

begin with Descartes. An Everyman volume contains his *Discourse on Method* and his other main works. He is quite readable. Unfortunately, Spinoza's famous *Ethics* (Everyman) is difficult, not only because of the difficulty of the thought, but also because of its strange presentation in the form of geometrical propositions. A short popular account of Spinoza's life and philosophy is given in J. A. Gunn's *Benedict Spinoza*. A more technical work is Leon Roth's *Spinoza*. John Locke's *Essay Concerning Human Understanding* is, of course, another philosophical landmark. Locke is far more readable than Spinoza. His work is the embodiment of English common sense, with all its strength and weakness. Leibniz's works are much more difficult, because of the intrinsic difficulty of his theories. A volume of his writings is included in the Everyman's Library Series. *Leibniz: The Monadology, etc.*, translated by R. Latta, with a long introduction on the philosopher's life and thought, contains all his important writings. Bertrand Russell's *The Philosophy of Leibniz* is a fine technical discussion which shows the importance of Leibniz for modern thought. Bishop Berkeley appears in the Everyman Library in the volume called *A New Theory of Vision and other Writings*. Berkeley is lucid. Two Everyman volumes give us David Hume's *A Treatise of Human Nature*, which has played so great a part in modern thought, and is fortunately written in a direct intelligible style.

Immanuel Kant is a very different kettle of fish. He is the most difficult, the most ponderous, the most self-contradictory, but according to some the most pregnant of modern philosophers. Others have regarded him as a philosophical disaster. His most famous work, *The Critique of Pure Reason*, translated by J. M. D. Meiklejohn (Bohn's Philosophical Library), was the supreme classic of modern philosophy throughout the long reign of philosophical Idealism. Innumerable books have been written about Kant's philosophy. The beginner should try A. D. Lindsay's little volume *The Philosophy of Immanuel Kant* (The People's Books). Use should also be made of the Modern Student's Library volume, *Kant, Selections*. The beginner should not attempt a serious attack on the *Critique* itself till he has ceased to be a beginner, and has read some of the later English Idealists. G. W. F. Hegel also is extremely difficult.

For some he is the last word in philosophy, for others he is an even worse disaster than Kant. His *Logic*, which is not really logic at all, but an exposition of Absolute Idealism, has played a great part not only in Idealism but as the inspiration of Marx's very different system. The more or less advanced beginner should at first be content with the Modern Student's Library volume, *Hegel, Selections*.

The development of philosophy since Hegel is most conveniently dealt with piecemeal, in connection with special subjects. I will mention here only the three main streams of recent philosophical thought, namely, Idealism, Pragmatism, and Realism. A valuable little introduction to modern Idealism is R. F. A. Hoernlé's *Idealism*. Serious students may pass on to F. H. Bradley's *Appearance and Reality*, a difficult but well-written classic. Pragmatism may be represented first by a paper on that subject in *Papers on Philosophy*, by William James (Everyman), and, for more detailed study, by James's *Pragmatism*. The best introduction to Realism is Russell's *Problems*, already mentioned. More detailed works will be cited later.

This is a convenient point to say that serious students who have time and persistent interest may find it useful to read, as occasion demands, the essays contained in the two volumes of *Contemporary British Philosophy* (Allen and Unwin), in which many well-known philosophers have summarised their theories.

Serious students will also find that in the course of their reading they are again and again referred to important philosophical studies in the *Proceedings* of the Aristotelian Society, and in issues of *Mind*, and of *Philosophy*, and other technical journals. These essays and reviews of philosophical books are much too specialised for beginners.

(d) *Specialisation.*—Let us suppose that the beginner has tackled Russell's *Problems*, or Joad's *Guide*, and Webb's little *History*. Let us suppose that he has also already embarked on a preliminary study of the great philosophers, with the aid of the Everyman volumes and others mentioned in the preceding section. He will have found his interest to some extent inclining in one direction rather than another. How is he to proceed? It is a good plan, I think, to continue one's general philosophical reading while also pursuing some particular theme with all possible thoroughness. Many readers, however, will not have time to devote to a two-fold plan of study. All they can do is to guard against undue specialisation by occasionally reading a general book; or against superficial catholicity by occasionally concentrating on their chosen theme.

I shall now make a few suggestions for reading in each of the main philosophical subjects. I shall always distinguish between elementary and more advanced works. So far as possible, but not invariably, I shall mention first, in each subject or subdivision of a subject, the shorter, easier books. Then I shall refer to a few more formidable technical works for the guidance of the minority who intend to become more than superficially acquainted with the particular subject.

Inevitably, the subjects have to be dealt with in some order. I follow in the main the sequence adopted in this book; but " Immortality " and " Mind and Body " are deposed from their leading place.

(e) *The External World and I.*—This subject has its origins in the work of Descartes, Locke, Berkeley and Hume. Berkeley's *Theory of Vision* is the historical root of the Idealist theory. For the Realist view the beginner, having referred to Russell's *Problems* and Joad's *Guide*, may attempt Russell's *Our Knowledge of the External World*. An interesting technical study by a modern Idealist is N. Kemp-Smith's *Prolegomena to an Idealist Theory of Knowledge*. On the Realist side, John Laird's *A Study in Realism* is attractively written. The serious student should also read G. E. Moore's famous paper, " The Refutation of Idealism," reprinted in his *Philosophical Studies*. Two American volumes (by various authors), *The New Realism* and *Essays in Critical Realism*, present respectively Realism without, and Realism with, the " mental act " and universals. Russell's *Analysis of Matter* is another very technical work. More recent and equally technical, though extraordinarily lucid, are C. D. Broad's *Perception, Physics and Reality* and his *Scientific Thought*. These two books contain a wealth of minute and illuminating criticism and original analysis. H. H. Price's *Perception* is a still more recent and highly technical classic.

The sceptical view of the Logical Positivists is very simply expressed in the course of the last chapter of A. J. Ayer's little *Language, Truth and Logic*, which all beginners and advanced students should read. They should also read Rudolf Carnap's two small classics, *The Unity of Science* and *Philosophy and Logical Syntax* (Psyche Miniatures).

(f) *Reasoning, its Nature and Scope.*—For the psychology of reasoning, W. Köhler's *The Mentality of Apes* is illuminating, and fascinating on its own account. Consult also any good text-book of psychology (see below, under Personality). E. Rignano's *The Psychology of Reasoning* is also helpful.

Those who are interested in formal logic will find W. S. Jevons's *Elementary Lessons in Logic* a useful little book. S. H. Mellone's *An Introductory Text-book of Logic* is fuller. H. W. B. Joseph's *Logic* is a bulky but well-written classic on the subject. Susan Stebbing's more recent *A Modern Introduction to Logic* is a very valuable but technical account of recent advances.

Idealism, Pragmatism, and Realism give very different accounts of the nature and validity of reason. Bernard Bosanquet's little book *The Essentials of Logic* gives the Idealist's interpretation. Bradley's *Appearance and Reality* contains a radical criticism of the power of human reason.

For Pragmatism, go to William James, the fountain head, and to the works referred to above. The serious student should pass on to read the whole of his book, *Pragmatism*. For a more subjectivistic version of Pragmatism read F. C. S. Schiller's *Humanism*.

In Bertrand Russell's *Mysticism and Logic* the title essay clearly distinguishes between the mystical and the rational points of view. There is also an important essay on the difference between " knowledge by acquaintance and knowledge by description."

For the controversy about universal characters, the reader should contrast Russell's early views in the *Problems* with his later views in *The Analysis of Mind*. The Idealist theory of the " concrete universal " is given in Chapter II of Bernard Bosanquet's *The Principle of Individuality and Value*, but is obscure. For the " distributive unity " of universals, read the last chapter of G. F. Stout's *Studies in Philosophy and Psychology*. This book contains other very helpful essays.

For the Logical Positivist's view of reasoning, the best intro-duction is Ayer's little book, already mentioned. Carnap's two small volumes in the Psyche Miniatures Series are important authoritative statements. Very serious students will find the origin of the subject in Wittgenstein's *Tractatus Logico-Philo-sophicus*. A technical critical study is J. R. Weinberg's *An Examination of Logical Positivism*. For the nature of mathematics, A. N. Whitehead's little book *Mathematics* (Home University Library) is invaluable. Russell's *Introduction to Mathematical Philosophy* is more difficult. L. Hogben's *Mathematics for the Million* is a mine of information.

(g) *Science and Philosophy.*—A. Wolf's *Essentials of Scientific Method* is a useful little textbook. A. D. Ritchie's *Scientific Method* is much fuller, more philosophical, and more technical. C. D. Broad's *Scientific Thought* (already mentioned) should be read by all serious students who seek a real understanding of recent movements of thought on this subject. A very different book is A. N. Whitehead's *Science and the Modern World,* which has had a widespread effect on the contemporary attitude to our modern, science-inspired culture. The book is rather uneven, but it is the most readable and perhaps the most stimulating of Whitehead's books. The same author's earlier books are important for any thorough study of the philosophy of science and of mathematics. *The Concept of Nature* contains much interesting matter on the abstracting of points and instants from our concrete experience.

The attitude to science which is implied in Dialectical Materialism is very briefly expounded in John Lewis's minute *Introduction to Philosophy* (New People's Library), and more fully in H. Levy's *A Philosophy for a Modern Man.*

Anyone interested in the relations of philosophy and science will probably have read some of the works of Sir Arthur Eddington and Sir James Jeans. These brilliant astronomers and able popularisers of science have found in recent physical theory evidence for an Idealist metaphysic. A. S. Eddington's Swarthmore Lecture (1929), *Science and the Unseen World,* states briefly the outline of his theory. His *The Nature of the Physical World* (1928), and *New Pathways in Science* (1934), besides containing much fascinating scientific information, present a more detailed account of his views on the limitations of science, and on indeterminacy in its relation to physics and to free will. Sir James Jeans's *The Universe Around Us* (1929) gives much illuminating science and some very doubtful philosophy. His *The Mysterious Universe* (1930) is a Pelican Book. A short expression on the other side by another and no less famous scientist is Max Planck's *Where is Science Going?* Philosophical criticism of Eddington and Jeans is given by C. E. M. Joad with his usual lucid style in his *Philosophical Aspects of Modern Science* (1932). Susan Stebbing's *Philosophy and the Physicists* (1937) is at present the last word in the matter. All who have been beguiled by the philosophy of the two famous astronomers should read this book. It is not only a detailed exposure of the philosophical errors of the two astronomers but also a sympathetic account of the revolution caused in science itself by the " uncertainty principle." In particular the principles of causality and probability are helpfully discussed.

(h) *The Irrational Determinants of Thought.*—On this subject the reader can consult, for the principle of distortion by unconscious motives, any modern psychological textbook (see below, under Personality), and for " social and economic determinants " he should read E. Westermarck's *Ethical Relativity* and any exposition of Marxism (see below, under Economic Determinism and Dialectical Materialism). For a general statement of the limitations of reason, and its relation to emotion, read John Macmurray's *Reason and Emotion.* See also the works on Bergson's philosophy, mentioned below, under Metaphysics.

(i) *Ethics.*—C. E. M. Joad's *Common Sense Ethics* is a very useful introduction. E. F. Carritt's *Morals and Politics* admirably summarises the classical theories, and also discusses political philosophy. For the psychology of moral experience read J. A. Hadfield's *Psychology and Morals.* For the growth of modern ethical theory, begin with J. S. Mill's *Utilitarianism* (Everyman's Library). A brief account of Idealist ethics will be found in J. H. Muirhead's *Elements of Ethics ;* a fuller textbook is J. S. Mackenzie's *Manual of Ethics.* For a criticism of Utilitarianism and a defence of intuition read G. E. Moore's *Ethics* (Home University Library), an example of minute logical analysis of moral experience. G. C. Field's *Moral Theory* gives an important criticism of Moore's position and is more readable. A valuable little book on the part played by reason in morality is Israel Levine's *Reason and Morals.* For ethical scepticism read E. Westermarck's *Ethical Relativity*, a very readable and cogent statement. This is a more bulky volume than those previously mentioned, but all students of ethics should read it. The

Logical Positivist's view is contained in Ayer's little book, already mentioned, and in Carnap's *Philosophy and Logical Syntax*.

Those who intend to make a serious study of ethics should read also C. D. Broad's *Five Types of Ethical Theory*, which discusses minutely and lucidly the ethical theories of Spinoza, Butler, Hume, Kant, and Sidgwick. They should also read, as the historical starting-point of the whole study, Aristotle's treatise called *The Nicomachean Ethics*. And they should study: for Hedonism, Henry Sidgwick's *The Methods of Ethics*; for the Idealist "self-fulfilment" theory, F. H. Bradley's *Ethical Studies*; for Idealism's "transcendence of good and evil," Chapter XXV of Bradley's *Appearance and Reality*; for a full defence of Intuitionism, G. E. Moore's *Principia Ethica*, which is minutely analytic. L. J. Hobhouse's *The Rational Good* is a very valuable criticism and development of the Idealist theory of moral obligation. A readable survey of the whole field of ethics, written from the Realist point of view, is John Laird's *A Study in Moral Theory*. A more recent careful survey of moral experience is L. A. Reid's *Creative Morality*.

(j) *Æsthetics.*—Though I have not had space to discuss æsthetic experience, I will mention one or two books on this difficult subject. Bernard Bosanquet's *Three Lectures on Æsthetics* states briefly the Idealist attitude. For a very different and more modern view read I. A. Richards's *The Principles of Literary Criticism.* Another valuable book is S. Alexander's *Art and the Material*. L. A. Reid's *A Study in Æsthetics* is a balanced survey of the whole field. Benedetto Croce's difficult *Æsthetic as Science of Expression* gives the view of the Neo-Idealists.

(k) *Personality.*—There are innumerable textbooks of psychology. In extra-mural classes I have found the following acceptable: A. E. Heath's very little volume *How We Behave* (W.E.A. Outlines), Susan S. Brierley's *An Introduction to Psychology*, R. S. Woodworth's *Psychology, A Study of Mental Life*. Useful also is Bernard Hart's little book *The Psychology of Insanity*. Another small and useful book is W. McDougall's *Psychology* (Home University Library). McDougall's *Outline of Psychology* is a much more advanced work, full of interesting, though sometimes controversial matter. Serious students should read, with a critical eye, J. B. Watson's *Psychology from the Point of View of a Behaviorist*. Sigmund Freud's famous *The Interpretation of Dreams* must also be read by serious students, who may then wish to pass on into the vast jungle of literature on psycho-analysis by Freud, Jung, Adler, and their followers. Such popular works as W. Trotter's *Instincts of the Herd in War and Peace*, and A. G. Tansley's *The New Psychology*, which were much discussed after the War, should be read with sharply critical intelligence. Those who are impressed by the un-doubted achievements of psycho-analysis and modern " instinct psychology " should read James Drever's *Instinct in Man*, a very thorough survey. For serious criticism of the whole matter they should make a point of reading the relevant chapters in G. C. Field's *Studies in Philosophy*. A slashing attack is given in A. Wohlgemuth's *Critical Examination of Psycho-analysis*. Ian Suttie's *Origins of Love and Hate* is a readable, temperate, and constructive criticism of psycho-analysis, though I have known it make an eminent psycho-analyst see red. It makes much of the distortion of modern thought by the " taboo on tenderness." Serious students should also read K. Koffka's *The Principles of Gestalt Psychology*. They may discover that some of the main principles of Gestalt Psychology were anticipated in G. F. Stout's classical *Manual of Psychology*. For the theory of senti-ments they should read A. F. Shand's *The Foundations of Char-acter*. For the diversity of character-types, C. G. Jung's *Psychological Types* is important. Joanna Field's *A Life of One's Own* is a delightful study of the sources of conscious motive. The *very* serious student should read Stout's big *Analytic Psychology* and James Ward's *Psychological Principles*. An interesting large volume on the evolution of mind is L. T. Hobhouse's *Mind in Evolution*. The most recent and impressive survey of the growth and present achievement of psychology is C. Spearman's *Psychology down the Ages*.

Those who are interested in the question of super-normal powers should read J. H. Rhine's *Extra-Sensory Perception*, J. W. Dunne's *An Experiment with Time*, and A. W. Osborn's *The Superphysical*. Whether all the claims put forward in these books will be finally established may still be doubted; but no serious student of human nature can afford to ignore them. The last deals with telepathy, pre-cognition, materialisation, telekinesis, survival, reincarnation, and mystical states. The fact that these subjects are still more or less "intellectually disreputable" makes it all the more important that the intellectually sincere student should take note of them.

On the relation between mind and body, read Henri Piéron's *Thought and the Brain* for a full technical statement of the materialist view. Bertrand Russell's *The Analysis of Mind* (1921) is a more philosophical study which has played an important part in the growth of ideas about the nature of mind. The most comprehensive, balanced, and lucid work on the general philosophy of mind, including the mind-body problem and survival and the structure of minds, is C. D. Broad's invaluable *The Mind and its Place in Nature* (1925).

(l) *Social Psychology and Social Philosophy.*—W. McDougall's *Introduction to Social Psychology* has played a great part in the evolution of modern psychology, but does not deal much with the social aspect. R. H. Thouless's *Social Psychology* is a textbook that should be read by all. Trotter and Tansley (mentioned above) must be treated with caution. A useful small book on the nature of society is G. D. H. Cole's *Social Theory*. R. M. Maciver's *Community* is an important larger work. McDougall's *The Group Mind* is a full-dress discussion of that difficult subject. Morris Ginsberg's *The Psychology of Society* is a brief survey which includes effective criticisms of the fashionable over-emphasis on instinct, and also of the Idealist theory of the State.

For Individualism, read J. S. Mill's *Utilitarianism* and his essay *On Liberty*. For the Idealist view, presumably Bernard Bosanquet's *The Philosophical Theory of the State* is the official English exposition. Serious students should read this and also L. T. Hobhouse's criticisms in his *The Metaphysical Theory of the State*. His *The Rational Good* (mentioned above) criticises the group-mind theory, as well as the Idealist theory of political obligation. Criticism of the Idealist political theory is also contained in E. F. Carritt's *Morals and Politics*.

For the three kinds of social mentality, read Gerald Heard's *The Ascent of Humanity*, the central idea of which is very significant, though for my part I suspect that the book "telescopes" the process of psychological evolution into *very* much too short a period. Also, he never makes it clear to me whether the pre-individual kind of consciousness is literally a group mind or simply an un-selfconscious way of experiencing on the part of the individual. The latter, I hope.

At this point it is appropriate to refer to the works of Professor John Macmurray, one of whose books has already been mentioned. I should describe his central theme as the contention that religion has become lifeless because it has ceased to be inspired by Christian friendship and the will for true community. Though I find his work sometimes ambiguous, I urge all readers to take note of his very significant books, *Creative Society* and *The Structure of Religious Experience*.

For a lucid and brief account of Economic Determinism read Part IV of John Strachey's excellent *The Theory and Practice of Socialism*. This book contains a useful Bibliographical Appendix on the literature of Marxism. G. D. H. Cole's *What Marx Really Meant* should also be read. Criticisms of Economic Determinism are contained in E. F. Carritt's little *Morals and Politics* and in Israel Levine's also little *Reason and Morals*. Serious students of Marxism will consult *A Handbook of Marxism* (Gollancz). Everyman's Library contains Karl Marx's *Capital*, in two volumes. For the moment I shall say no more on this subject, as it is more conveniently treated under the later heading of Dialectical Materialism.

(m) *Metaphysics*.—The Introduction to Bradley's *Appearance and Reality* claims to be a defence of metaphysical enquiry, but the upshot of his kind of Absolute Idealism is that human reason is incapable of making fully true propositions about reality. The Introduction to Broad's *Scientific Thought* distinguishes between " critical " and " speculative " philosophy, and points out that the latter is mostly guess-work. The Logical Positivist's view is, as usual, clearly explained in Ayer's *Language, Truth and Logic*, and in Carnap's two little books. A much more technical account occurs in Weinberg's *Examination of Logical Positivism*.

I have already referred to the works of the great modern metaphysical philosophers, Descartes, Spinoza, Leibniz, Kant, Hegel. A brief survey of modern metaphysical thought is C. E. M. Joad's *Mind and Matter*. R. F. A. Hoernlé's *Idealism* is also relevant here. For a thorough study of metaphysical Idealism serious students, but not beginners, should read, besides

Appearance and Reality, T. H. Green's *Prolegomena to Ethics*, and Bernard Bosanquet's *The Principle of Individuality and Value*. By far the most precise and technically brilliant study in Idealist metaphysics is J. McT. E. McTaggart's *The Nature of Existence*. This famous work is an amazing logical structure based on premises which some readers will feel to be inadequate. C. D. Broad has written an important *Examination of McTaggart's Philosophy*. Those who wish to study Italian Neo-Idealism should read H. Wildon Carr's *The Philosophy of Benedetto Croce*, and then, if they are prepared for difficult stuff, they may pass on to Croce's four-volume *The Philosophy of Spirit*, and to Giovanni Gentile's *The Theory of Mind as Pure Act*.

For Realist criticism of Idealist metaphysics the reader should consult Bertrand Russell's works, already mentioned. For a comprehensive account of his own recent position, read his *An Outline of Philosophy*. S. Alexander's *Space, Time and Deity* is an impressive Realist metaphysical system. For the foundations of philosophical materialism, and also for the early influence of biological ideas, the serious student must study Herbert Spencer's *Synthetic Philosophy*. A very interesting commentary on him, and also on the relations of Dialectical Materialism and biology, is contained in Joseph Needham's short Herbert Spencer Lecture, called *Integrative evels: A Revaluation of the Idea of Progress*.

For Dialectical Materialism the reader should study (in addition to the works referred to under Economic Determinism) the brief exposition and criticism in Joad's *Guide*; but he should also study the works of the Dialectical Materialists themselves. He might begin with John Lewis's *Textbook of Marx's Philosophy*, and pass on to *Aspects of Dialectical Materialism*, a co-operative volume by H. Levy and others. He should certainly read H. Levy's *A Philosophy for a Modern Man*. This volume contains a brilliant analysis of the appearance of new qualities in scientific fields of study, and a striking account of social evolution. Philosophically, however, it seems to me to be rather obscure and ambiguous about the basic ideas of Dialectical Materialism.

For an introduction to Bergson, the beginner will find J. A. Gunn's *Bergson and his Philosophy* a useful summary. H. Wildon Carr's *The Philosophy of Change* is a more technical study. Translations of Bergson's famous books bear the titles *Time and Free Will*, *Matter and Memory*, *Creative Evolution* (the most famous), and *Mind Energy*. The theory of Emergence is given in C. Lloyd Morgan's *Emergent Evolution*. S. Alexander's *Space, Time and Deity* also makes use of Emergence. For A. N. Whitehead's philosophy, the beginner should read *Science and the Modern World*, omitting the more technical chapters. Whitehead's main metaphysical work is *Process and Reality*, which is very difficult, but full of thought-provoking matter.

On the special subject of Time, the beginner should first grasp the observable characteristics of ordinary temporal experience, as described, for instance, in Stout's *Manual of Psychology*, Book III, Chapter V. Modern ideas about time are largely derived from Bergson's works (mentioned above). The serious student should read, in the philosophical journal *Mind*, 1908, p. 457, and 1909, p. 343, two important articles by McTaggart. The subject is also, of course, discussed in his *The Nature of Existence*, mentioned above. C. D. Broad's *Scientific Thought* contains criticisms of McTaggart's views, together with important ideas of his own. Dunne's *An Experiment with Time* and Osborn's *The Superphysical* should, of course, be read for supernormal temporal experience.

Mystical experience, also, is discussed by Osborn. The most comprehensive and readable survey is Evelyn Underhill's *Mysticism*. Rudolf Otto's *The Idea of the Holy* is a short book which stresses awe as an element in religious experience, and is important as a corrective to the much commoner idea that the essence of religion is the conviction of the deity's friendliness. A sceptical, yet in a sense curiously mystical, attitude, reminiscent of Spinoza's " intellectual love of God," is admirably expressed in G. Santayana's *Platonism and the Spiritual Life*. Bertrand Russell's *Religion and Science* (Home University Library) is a concise summary of the sceptical view of religion. All who are interested in the psychology of religion should read William James's classic, *The Varieties of Religious Experience*. A useful and brief modern survey is R. H. Thouless's *An Introduction to the Psychology of Religion*.

(n) *Practical Upshot.*—I will close by mentioning some books, of very different types, which have influenced me in forming ideas about the crisis of the modern world. I am conscious that, though for one reason or another all of them seem to me valuable, their authors are in some respects strongly opposed to one another. Stephen Spender's *Forward from Liberalism*, though rather hastily written, is a sincere expression of the author's gradual discovery that the old political doctrines were insufficient. John Strachey's *The Theory and Practice of Socialism* (mentioned above) is a brilliant account of the case for far-reaching social change. G. D. H. Cole's *The People's Front* urges combined action by all progressive forces to preserve democracy. Complementary to these exhortations to political action is Aldous Huxley's *Ends and Means*, which, though I regard a good deal of it as very questionable, does stress the fundamental importance of the free critical intelligence, of kindliness, and of individual responsibility. John Macmurray's *Creative Society* and *The Structure of Religious Experience*, already mentioned, are important because they stress the fact that religion must be base if it fails to issue in vigorous action to create a better social order. Naomi Mitchison's *The Moral Basis of Politics* is a sincere and unconventional attempt to lay bare the fundamental motives of moral and political action, and to consider dispassionately the moral aims both of Fascists and Socialists. She seeks to combine the spirit of sympathetic understanding of the more reputable motives of Fascists with the spirit of uncompromising resistance to the attack on our liberties.

POSTSCRIPT

Since this appendix went to press the following books have appeared, all of which are relevant to one or other aspect of our theme: L. Hogben's *Science for the Citizen*, C. E. M. Joad's *Guide to the Philosophy of Morals*, G. N. M. Tyrrell's *Science and Psychical Phenomena*, J. B. S. Haldane's *The Marxist Philosophy and the Sciences*, Bertrand Russell's *Power, a New Social Analysis*, Christopher Caudwell's *Studies in a Dying Culture*, John Macmurray's *The Clue to History*.

INDEX

Note.—This Index does not cover the Appendix.

INDEX

Freedom of expression, 296
Freud, S., 192 f., 249

Gentile, G., 364
God, 32 f., 87, 127 f., 328, 330 f., 337, 340, 349, 393 f., 418, 427
Good, Meaning of, 172, 184, 205
Group Mind theory, 270, 274 f.

Heard, G., 278
Hedonism, 171, 174 f., 208
Hegel, G. W., 268, 272, 304 f., 355, 404
Herd-mentality, 278 f., 320, 430, 433
Hume, D., 57, 87 f., 94, 174, 225, 253 f., 260

Idea, 127
Idealism, 84, 99, 135, 172, 268, 301 f., 346 f., 353 f., 413
Illusion, 80, 94 f., 99, 101
Implication, 120 f.
Indeterminacy, 145 f., 148 f., 367
Individualism, 264 f., 281 f.
Individuality, 431
Instants, 406
Instinct, 237, 242 f., 251 f., 381 f., 384
Intellect, 113 f., 239, 243, 255, 381
Intelligence, 114 f.
Interactionism, 54 f., 58 f.
Intuition, 30 f., 117, 161, 164 f., 174, 184 f., 381 f., 414
Irrationalism, 158 f., 346

James, W., 111, 227, 261
Jeans, J., 148, 151

Kant, I., 88 f., 121, 178 f., 268, 325, 353 f.
Köhler, W., 114, 226 f., 232

Laissez faire, 265 f., 431 f.
Language, 328
Left, The Political, 441
Leibniz, 339, 347 f., 388
Lenin, 313, 318, 425
Levy, H., 313, 374

Liberalism, 431 f.
Life Force, 79, 85 f., 88, 94, 115, 353
Locke, J., 85 f., 94, 99, 353

Marx, K., 272, 307 f., 313, 369 f., 381
Materialism, 152; Dialectical, 307, 315 f., 364, 369 f.; Mechanical, 364 f., 372
Matter, 382, 391, 405 f.
Mechanism, 146, 385, 387
Memory, 229 f., 231
Metaphysics, 325 f.; defined, 84
Mill, J. S., 105, 178
Mohammed, 425
Monads, 349 f.
Monism, 134, 160, 164, 268 f., 340 f., 347, 353 f., 365 f., 367, 390 f., 401; Neutral, 100
Moore, G. E., 176, 184, 201
Morgan, C. Lloyd, 385
Motion, 382 f., 410
Mutations, 379
Mysticism, 32, 166, 209, 255 f., 414 f., 424

Nature, Uniformity of, 143
Necessity, 37 f., 115 f., 145, 150, 351, 374
Need, 235 f.
Needham, J., 308
Nominalism, 129
Non-violence, 440
Novelty, 199, 242, 322, 373 f., 379
Number, 124, 141 f.

Organic whole, 226, 229
Organism, 357 f., 365 f., 388 f.
Osborn, A. W., 44

Parallelism, 67 f., 342
Parties, political, 442
Perception, 79 f., 231
Perfection, 127 f., 336 f.
Personality, 32 f., 207, 211, 221 f., 402 f.
Phenomenalism, 87 f., 99, 103
Plato, 127 f., 173 f., 347, 393

463

PENGUIN BOOKS

COMPLETE LIST OF PUBLICATIONS TO AUGUST 1939

FICTION   *orange covers*

Richard Aldington	*The Colonel's Daughter*
" Bartimeus "	*A Tall Ship*
Vicki Baum	*Helene*
Hilaire Belloc	*But Soft: We Are Observed*
Arnold Bennett	*Grand Babylon Hotel*
Ambrose Bierce	*In the Midst of Life*
Algernon Blackwood	*The Centaur*
Phyllis Bottome	*Private Worlds*
Ernest Bramah	*Kai Lung's Golden Hours*
	The Wallet of Kai Lung
Ann Bridge	*Peking Picnic*
D. K. Broster	*Sir Isumbras at the Ford*
Joanna Cannan	*High Table*
G. K. Chesterton	*Man Who Was Thursday*
Norman Collins	*Penang Appointment*
Susan Ertz	*Madame Claire*
	Now East, Now West
William Faulkner	*Soldiers' Pay*
E. M. Forster	*A Passage to India*
Leonhard Frank	*Carl and Anna*
Crosbie Garstin	*The Owls' House*
Stella Gibbons	*Cold Comfort Farm*
Louis Golding	*Store of Ladies*
Ian Hay	*" Pip "*
	A Safety Match
Constance Holme	*The Lonely Plough*
Claude Houghton	*Chaos is Come Again*
	I Am Jonathan Scrivener
W. W. Jacobs	*Deep Waters*
	Many Cargoes
M. R. James	*Ghost Stories of an Antiquary*
Stephen Leacock	*Literary Lapses*
Sinclair Lewis	*Mantrap*
Rose Macaulay	*Crewe Train*
Denis Mackail	*Greenery Street*
Ethel Mannin	*Children of the Earth*
	Ragged Banners
R. H. Mottram	*The Spanish Farm*
D. Kilham Roberts	*Penguin Parade (1)*
(editor)	*Penguin Parade (2)*
	Penguin Parade (3)
	Penguin Parade (4)
	Penguin Parade (5)
	Penguin Parade (6)
E. Arnot Robertson	*Ordinary Families*
V. Sackville-West	*The Edwardians*
Antoine de Saint-Exupéry	*Night Flight*
Rafael Sabatini	*Bardelys the Magnificent*

Saki	*Selected Stories of Saki*
William Saroyan	*The Daring Young Man*
Olive Schreiner	*Story of an African Farm*
Ramon Sender	*Seven Red Sundays*
Graham Seton	*The W Plan*
Beatrice Kean Seymour	*Youth Rides Out*
Edward Shanks	*(2 vols.) Queer Street*
Ignazio Silone	*Fontamara*
Osbert Sitwell	*Before the Bombardment*
Somerville and Ross	
	Some Experiences of an Irish R.M.
Alan Steele (editor)	
	Selected Modern Short Stories (1)
	Selected Modern Short Stories (2)
Ralph Straus	*Unseemly Adventure*
Tchehov	*Tales from Tchehov*
Angela Thirkell	*Wild Strawberries*
E. Temple Thurston	
	The City of Beautiful Nonsense
Edward Thompson	*An Indian Day*
Ben Travers	*A Cuckoo in the Nest*
Doreen Wallace	*Barnham Rectory*
Hugh Walpole	*Mr. Perrin and Mr. Traill*
Evelyn Waugh	*Black Mischief*
	Decline and Fall
	Vile Bodies
Edith Wharton	*Ethan Frome*
Antonia White	*Frost in May*
P. G. Wodehouse	*My Man Jeeves*
Francis Brett Young	*The Crescent Moon*

CRIME FICTION

green covers

Margery Allingham	*Police at the Funeral*
Anthony Armstrong	*Ten Minute Alibi*
H. C. Bailey	*Mr. Fortune, Please*
E. C. Bentley	*Trent's Last Case*
Anthony Berkeley	*The Piccadilly Murder*
Alice Campbell	*Spider Web*
John Dickson Carr	*It Walks by Night*
	The Waxworks Murder
Agatha Christie	*The Murder on the Links*
	The Mysterious Affair at Styles
G. D. H. and Margaret Cole	
	Murder at Crome House
J. J. Connington	*The Dangerfield Talisman*
	Death at Swaythling Court
	The Murder in the Maze

CONTINUED

A. Conan Doyle *Hound of the Baskervilles*
J. Jefferson Farjeon *No. 17*
John Ferguson *The Man in the Dark*
Richard Keverne *The Havering Plot*
The Man in the Red Hat
The Sanfield Scandal
Missing from his Home
C. H. B. Kitchin *Death of My Aunt*
Philip Macdonald *The Rasp*
Ngaio Marsh *Enter a Murderer*
A Man Lay Dead
J. C. Masterman *An Oxford Tragedy*
A. A. Milne *The Red House Mystery*
Gladys Mitchell *Death at the Opera*
John Rhode *The House on Tollard Ridge*
The Murders in Praed Street
Sax Rohmer *The Mystery of Dr. Fu-Manchu*
Dorothy L. Sayers *Documents in the Case*
W. Stanley Sykes *The Missing Moneylender*
Henry Wade *The Verdict of You All*
Edgar Wallace *The Four Just Men*
H. G. Wells *The Invisible Man*

TRAVEL & ADVENTURE *cerise covers*

J. Johnston Abraham *The Surgeon's Log*
Edmund Blunden *Undertones of War*
F. S. Chapman *Watkins' Last Expedition*
Apsley Cherry-Garrard
(2 vols.) *The Worst Journey in the World*
Alexandra David-Neel
With Mystics and Magicians in Tibet
Gandar Dower *Amateur Adventure*
A. J. Evans *The Escaping Club*
Anthony Fokker *Flying Dutchman*
Rosita Forbes *From Red Sea to Blue Nile*
Alain Gerbault *Fight of the Firecrest*
Anne Morrow Lindbergh
North to the Orient
Martin Lindsay *Sledge*
David Scott *The Egypt's Gold*
Captain von Rintelen *The Dark Invader*
Nora Waln *House of Exile*

MISCELLANEOUS *yellow covers*

Earl Baldwin *On England*
Francis and Vera Meynell (editors)
(2 vols.) *The Week-end Book*
Alexander Woollcott *While Rome Burns*

BIOGRAPHY & MEMOIRS *dark blue covers*

H. C. Armstrong *Grey Steel (J. C. Smuts)*
Grey Wolf (Mustafa Kemal)
Lord of Arabia (Ibn Saud)
E. F. Benson *As We Were*
L. E. O. Charlton *" Charlton "*
John Fothergill *An Innkeeper's Diary*
Pamela Frankau *I Find Four People*
Stephen Gwynn *Captain Scott*
B. H. Liddell Hart *(2 vols.) Foch*
Ethel Mannin *Confessions and Impressions*
André Maurois *Ariel*
Disraeli
George Moore *Confessions of a Young Man*
Maurice O'Sullivan *20 Years A-Growing*

DRAMA *red covers*

BACK TO METHUSELAH, Bernard Shaw
FOUR PLAYS by A. A. Milne
THE PENGUIN SHAKESPEARE, edited by Dr. G. B. Harrison ; these plays, each in a separate volume with special Notes and Introductions, are available so far :

Twelfth Night *Henry the Fifth*
Hamlet *As You Like It*
King Lear *A Midsummer Night's Dream*
The Tempest *The Merchant of Venice*
Richard II *Romeo and Juliet*
Julius Caesar *Henry IV (part 1)*
Macbeth *Henry IV (part 2)*
Othello *Much Ado About Nothing*
The Sonnets *Antony and Cleopatra*
SEVEN FAMOUS ONE-ACT PLAYS, by Alfred Sutro, A. P. Herbert, Clifford Bax, Stanley Houghton, W. W. Jacobs, J. A. Ferguson and Oliphant Down.

PENGUIN GUIDES

Edited by L. Russell Muirhead, with 8-page section of Bartholomew's 3-colour maps.

KENT, SUSSEX AND SURREY
SOMERSET
CORNWALL
DEVON
DERBYSHIRE
LAKE DISTRICT
Others to follow.

CONTINUED

ILLUSTRATED CLASSICS

Art Director : Robert Gibbings;
Introductions by G. B. Harrison

Jane Austen   Pride and Prejudice
(illustrated by Helen Binyon)
Robert Browning   Selected Poems
(Iain Macnab)
Daniel Defoe   (2 vols.) Robinson Crusoe
(J. R. Biggs)
Richard Jefferies   The Story of My Heart
(Gertrude Hermes)
Herman Melville Typee (Robert Gibbings)
Edgar Allan Poe
Some Tales of Mystery and Imagination
(Douglas Percy Bliss)
Laurence Sterne   A Sentimental Journey
(Gwen Raverat)
Jonathan Swift   Gulliver's Travels
(Theodore Naish)
David Thoreau Walden (Ethelbert White)

PENGUIN SPECIALS

Norman Angell   The Great Illusion—Now
Norman Angell & Dorothy Frances Buxton
You and the Refugee
The Duchess of Atholl Searchlight on Spain
F. Borkenau   The New German Empire
Phyllis Bottome   The Mortal Storm
S. Grant Duff   Europe and the Czechs
G. T. Garratt   Mussolini's Roman Empire
Louis Golding   *The Jewish Problem
Konrad Heiden One Man Against Europe
C. E. M. Joad   Why War ?
F. Elwyn Jones   The Attack from Within
Richard Keane (editor)
Germany—What Next ?
F. Le Gros Clark and Richard M. Titmuss
Our Food Problem
Stefan Lorant   I Was Hitler's Prisoner
E. O. Lorimer   What Hitler Wants
Mass-Observation   Britain
Edgar Mowrer
Germany Puts the Clock Back
Mowrer in China
P E P Report   Britain's Health
J. M. D. Pringle and Marthe Rajchman
China Struggles for Unity
W. J. Rose   Poland
Wickham Steed   The Press

PELICAN SPECIALS

Arnold Bennett   Literary Taste
Anthony Bertram   *Design
Arnold Haskell   *Ballet
Robert Gibbings *Blue Angels & Whales
Lucia Moholy
A Hundred Years of Photography
Hugh Nicol   *Microbes by the Million

PELICAN BOOKS
light blue covers

F. L. Allen   *(2 vols.) Only Yesterday
Clive Bell   Civilisation
Lady Bell   The Letters of Gertrude Bell
G. D. H. Cole   Practical Economics
Socialism in Evolution
J. G. Crowther
*(2 vols.) An Outline of the Universe
Dobrée and Manwaring
The Floating Republic
J. H. Fabre *Social Life in the Insect World
Sigmund Freud   Totem and Taboo
Psychopathology of Everyday Life
Roger Fry   Vision and Design
Bishop Gore   Belief in God
J. B. S. Haldane   The Inequality of Man
Élie Halévy A History of the English People
(4 vols.)
J. L. and Barbara Hammond
Lord Shaftesbury
G. B. Harrison   *Introducing Shakespeare
(editor) A Book of English Poetry
Julian Huxley   Essays in Popular Science
Julian Huxley, A. C. Haddon and A. M.
Carr-Saunders   *We Europeans
Sir James Jeans   *The Mysterious Universe
P. Kropotkin   Mutual Aid
R. S. Lambert (editor)   *Art in England
H. J. Laski   Liberty in the Modern State
H. J. and Hugh Massingham (editors)
(2 vols.) The Great Victorians
W. J. Perry   The Growth of Civilisation
Eileen Power   *Medieval People
D. K. Roberts (editor)
(2 vols.) The Century's Poetry
Bernard Shaw
(2 vols.) The Intelligent Woman's Guide
Olaf Stapledon   Last and First Men
L. Susan Stebbing
Thinking to Some Purpose
J. W. N. Sullivan   Limitations of Science
The Bases of Modern Science
R. H. Tawney
Religion and the Rise of Capitalism
Beatrice Webb (2 vols.) My Apprenticeship
Josiah Wedgwood
The Economics of Inheritance
H. G. Wells A Short History of the World
A. N. Whitehead
Science and the Modern World
Leonard Woolf   After the Deluge
Virginia Woolf   The Common Reader
Sir Leonard Woolley *Ur of the Chaldees
*Digging up the Past

* ILLUSTRATED